SACRED MARCHING ORDERS

*Igniting the Solar Feminine
at the Dawn of a New Age*

Patricia Fero

ISBN 978-0-9767932-2-9

1. Spirituality   2. Women's issues   3. Self-help

Patricia Fero
3830 Packard St., Ste 250
Ann Arbor, MI 48108
(734) 973-0817
Email: pat_fero@yahoo.com
Website: www.patriciafero.com

ALSO BY PATRICIA FERO

What Happens When Women Wake Up?
Mining for Diamonds

To Marie...
Alpha Female Extraordinaire

Contents

Gratitude

As this book begins within the nurturing energy of the lunar feminine, so did the editing process begin in the unconditional love, acceptance, and lunar listening of Jeanie De Rousseau. We spent every Sunday morning marinating in the energies of the beautifully edited interviews Jeanie had crafted.

She immersed herself in the truth of the words offered by the 20 women who each spoke powerfully from their Core Essence Selves. The energies of these women are woven throughout this book. I thank all of you for your willingness to share your truth and power with me. This is the fertile soil from which this solar feminine manual burst forth.

My journey into the solar feminine began with Lucia Rene. Her book, Unplugging the Patriarchy, offered the definition of the solar feminine, which had been coined by Celia Fenn in 2005. Lucia's embodiment of the solar feminine activated a spark within me which burst forth in the creation of this book. Both Lucia and Celia have played enormous roles in reversing the trajectory of patriarchy on our precious earth.

My next expression of gratitude goes to Charlon Bobo, my editor, who marched forth powerfully with me as she showed up for the extraordinary activation of the solar feminine within her. As she did this, we created a synergy that powerfully fueled this energy within both of us and the book. I thank Charlon for the adventure of rewriting this book in the service of the solar feminine.

As I handed the project over to Jeanne Bedard for formatting and graphic design she also became activated by the energy and jumped in—full powered—into the solar feminine. She created a perfect visual expression of solar feminine power.

Watching and particiapating with Vikki Hanchin in her breathtaking process of stepping into her power so fully — with passionate commitment to the planet—is inherent in these pages.

Lauri Keller's powerful intuitive listening and profound questions were a part of our daily routine. This process continued to deepen as my writing became progressively stronger and more clear. Lauri has been a consistent and receptive container for my expression.

I thank *Gather the Women* (GTW) for the most welcoming embrace into the Divine Feminine. Calling Marilyn Nyborg and connecting with this group powerfully supported my immersion into my purpose. GTW activated my role as catalyst for igniting the collective feminine in planetary awakening.

It is completely impossible for me to convey my gratitude for my extraordinary circle of powerful women. You all know who you are and how much I love you. Without all of you this book would not have been written.

Editor's Note

In the process of book writing or editing, it is consistently true that the content rewrites us; sometimes lightly, sometimes profoundly, but transforming us, nevertheless. As an editor I have come to rely on this dynamic. It is so reliable that I even look forward to it.

In the case of *Sacred Marching Orders*, before the project officially began, I told a friend that I would look back on this book as one of the most memorable and life-altering manuscripts of my life.

I was grateful for this fore-knowing because it gave me an opportunity to be truly conscious as the shift in me began. With a wink of my eye and an agreeable nod to the Universe,

I said, "I hear you. I feel the magnitude and importance of this work. With fierce surrender to my own plan, in service to all humanity, I am willing.

Whatever lies ahead, I am not afraid. I was born for this." Obviously, I was not speaking to the task of merely editing a manuscript. This was so much more.

As the project commenced, I became the solar awakening editor. My first self-appointed mission was to purchase a pair of vintage combat boots, circa 1965–the year of my birth. As abstract as it seemed initially, and as time would reveal, this solar action served to infuse this book with the necessary action-orientation and unwavering commitment required of any woman who awakens; the willingness to be the model of the solar feminine; to live it; to be in active and willing collaboration during the process; to stand in firm resolve, regardless of external circumstances.

I spent many hours on the march, wearing those boots,

directed by my sacred marching orders–back and forth in my office–to allow the perfect words and vibration to flow through me as a catalyst for global change. Those boots serve to remind each of us of the responsibility in these auspicious times to become those women to whom other women can map.

In service to you, I went first. Now it's your turn. May this book awaken the solar feminine in you in a way that transforms and rewrites you in the process.

Get on your boots, girls; it's time to march.

Bursting forth,

Charlon Bobo

"Building pathways, strengthening channels, and raising vibration comes from discipline, focus, and attention."

– Nenie Beanie

SACRED
MARCHING
ORDERS

Igniting the Solar Feminine
at the Dawn of a New Age

Patricia Fero

" *I am not afraid. I was born for this.*"
– JOAN OF ARC

Invitation

As the author of three books, I am convinced that the book-writing process has its own guiding wisdom; a way of taking us where it wants us to go; magically and powerfully rewriting us in the process.

When I began writing *Sacred Marching Orders* in the Fall of 2009, I was unfamiliar with the term solar feminine. My understanding was that the divine—or sacred—feminine was exclusively the lunar feminine. The qualities of receptivity, nurturing, inclusiveness, and powerful listening were all I knew of the feminine.

Introduced to the concept of the solar feminine in Lucia Rene"s book, *Unplugging the Patriarchy,* she describes it this way, "The solar feminine embodies yang energy, strength, passion, creativity, and action—qualities that have not been appreciated in females since the matrilineal era of some 6,000 years ago." She continued, "The solar feminine is quite different from the lunar feminine whose yin energies—gentle and receptive, and nurturing—were the only type of femininity that has been accepted through the Patriarchal Age."

I was captivated by these words and realize in retrospect that with this new awareness, a spark was ignited in me. And the spark was fanned by my increasing contact with Lucia, who wholly embodies the solar feminine.

As I made the final edits on this book, my own solar awakening occurred. It burst forth powerfully and quite unexpectedly, necessitating a complete rewrite of the original manuscript to feature the solar feminine. Starting as a lunar, oxytocin-laced elixir of comfort and gentleness, as a direct result of my personal activation, this manuscript morphed into the solar orb of illumination you now hold in your hands.

This book was written in the service of putting the solar feminine on the map: square, dead center, in the middle of the map to be exact, center stage, full blown, spotlight blazing.

The solar feminine must be center-stage right now because she has been absent, invisible for the last 5,000 years. The lunar has gone too far into passivity, dependence, and ineffectiveness. Just as the dark side of the masculine has gone awry under patriarchy—aggression, dominance, control, manipulation, over-valuing the head over the heart—men need to reclaim their lunar masculine. But we'll leave that in their very capable hands. As women, we need to reclaim our solar feminine.

Celia Fenn, who coined the term "solar feminine," writes, "To embody the solar is to be strong, passionate, creative, and energetic." We need to embody these characteristics right now because it's the next necessary step in the evolution of humanity.

This book begins with the lunar feminine because this is an energy with which we women have a high level of comfort. We see it as our native land. The lunar feminine has been our primary mode of functioning under patriarchal rule. It is our default mechanism. The solar feels new, unfamiliar, and even dangerous to us. In fact, it is very dangerous to maintaining the status quo. Releasing the old and creating and embodying the new is often a frightening process. However, the more we do it, and the more of us that do it, the easier it becomes.

Teachers like Sharon Maynard and Lucia Rene have awakened an ancient knowing that power is truly our birthright as a woman. This truth was decimated under patriarchal reign. Centuries of subjugation of women—through countless methods of violence and mind control—have convinced us to relinquish our power.

I see it in myself consistently. Beginning this book process in the energies of the lunar feminine rather than bursting forth powerfully in the energies of the solar feminine is a painful example of my propensity to quiet my voice in the service of compromise, safety, and cooperation. Maybe you do the same.

In my last book, *What Happens When Women Wake Up?*, I wrote about women who walk ahead, as scouts, to clear the path for others to follow. The opportunity is here, now, for us who have the courage to step into our power and embody the solar feminine. We become templates for others to embrace this powerful, crucial energy at this time of planetary urgency.

I walk ahead to show you the way. I march forth into this new terrain having learned many hard lessons by too much yielding and compromising, too little standing in my own power, and too seldom speaking in my own voice without apology.

It's a new world for all of us. As never before, there is divine assistance available to us to be used in the service of all life. To that end, may this book ignite the solar feminine within you and spur you to action.

Illuminating the path,

Patricia Fero

"*Heaven is an energy from the inside. The more you allow yourself to experience it, the deeper or higher you go.*"
– NENIE BEANIE

The Lunar Feminine

What is the Lunar Feminine?

When I began writing my second book, *What Happens When Women Wake Up?*, I had never heard the phrase, Divine Feminine. That experience launched me into a crash course of learning about the Lunar Feminine which, at that time, was also termed Divine Feminine. I devoured books that featured the divine feminine and lived immersed in that energy.

During that time I discovered *Gather the Women Global Matrix* and became a regional coordinator. My enthusiasm for the lunar was unbounded. At my first regional coordinator's conference, I met my mentor Jean Shinoda Bolen, whose writings are based in Jungian-Feminism. I was ecstatic. Jean sat with us in circle all day. My first experience with circle was deep and profound. I felt like I had come home for the first time.

Immediately I began organizing circles in my community. I developed retreats and workshops, and created the process of *Essence-to-Essence Conversation*, which is the circle process conducted in dyads. I heard the word "oxytocin" (the nurturing hormone) for the first time and fell in love with the experience of living immersed in a world of nurturing, inclusive, and receptive women.

I connected in profound ways with women all over the country and we remained connected via regular telephone conversations. Most of them were *Gather the Women* Regional Coordinators, and most had been immersed in the lunar feminine for decades. They were the most welcoming community of women imaginable.

I was ripe for experiencing the qualities of the lunar feminine. I worked on a project called *Women Waking the World* in which we defined, described, and proclaimed feminine, lunar qualities. The qualities that are traditionally defined as lunar are:

1. receptivity
2. nurturing
3. responsiveness
4. inclusiveness
5. deep, profound listening

My immersion in—and love affair with—the lunar feminine was powerful and it is the basis—the fertile ground—from which this book germinated. And I affirm that it is the solid foundation upon which many creative endeavors are given birth.

What is the Value of the Lunar Feminine?

The value of the lunar feminine cannot be overestimated or overstated. This book features the solar feminine because it is new to us, crucial at this time on the planet, and carries our severed roots.

However, the lunar embodies receptivity, nurturing, inclusiveness, and deep profound listening. It is this powerful listening that yielded the following prophetic dreams and inform us of the dire need—and ultimate return of the feminine—that is the key to our current transition.

Julie's dream breaks open our hearts and offers hope.

Lynda's dream shows us the indigenous grandmothers emerging from the forest to lead us forward.

Vikki's dream is a continuation of Lynda's—showing us the gathering, mobilizing, and celebration of the feminine as we usher in the New World.

Beth's vision provides a powerful visual of encasing the planet in a net-light of healing, reminding us of our Oneness.

There are no greater examples of the power and importance of the lunar feminine than these lunar dreams and visions.

"Nothing is more important than raising your vibration."
– NENIE BEANIE

• Severed Roots
Julie Raymond's Dream

I'm standing beside a tree. I become aware that there is something, a life force, trapped beneath the soil. I find a hole and crawl down into it. It's very tight, like I'm trying to crawl through a rabbit's warren. It feels like a birth passage.

I reach a place where I can see a woman lying in the fetal position; she is emaciated, horribly emaciated. She has long hair, and she's talking, but I can't hear her because she is so frail. It's very cramped quarters, but I place my face next to hers, and I hear her say, "Get me out of here." It is a declarative, intense statement—not calm, more like a command—and her voice is quivering with pent-up emotion.

The roots of the tree are growing through her body because she has been there so long. I want to assist her. I immediately begin cutting away the roots, and then I pick her up and hold her in my arms while I crawl out of the hole.

When I get out, there are women—hundreds of them—walking in a giant circle. I have no idea where they came from. Some of them are singing, some are chanting, and some are drumming. But they are all carrying something different, something unique.

By this point when I get to the surface, I'm not carrying the woman anymore. She has dissolved into the pieces that these women are carrying. I realize that every woman carries a part of our lost heritage, our secrets. We are each depositories of something precious that is important in our collective healing.

Reflections on the dream: Julie's vision catapults us into an awareness of the desperate condition of the abandoned

"Mother." As she brings her to the surface into the Light, she is shown the image of each of us carrying our unique piece that returns her to her magnificence.

She is REMEMBERED through each of us.

• Return of the Indigenous Soul
Lynda Terry's Dream

I am someplace either visiting or living/staying with other women. Without specifics, I know that something has happened outside of where we are (meaning: in the town or region)—a crisis of some sort or maybe a death. I hear a sound in the distance—a cross between a hum and a buzz. It grows louder. With others, I go outside, to the side of the road, drawn to seek the source of the sound. To our left, perhaps the equivalent of a block away, the road ends at a forest. The sound is clearly coming from the forest. The sound grows in volume. Although never overwhelmingly loud, I feel its vibration inside my body, as well as hearing it, and I know that something big is about to happen. It seems others know this, too.

As we watch and wait, we see large numbers of indigenous women of many cultures emerging from within the woods to its edge and onto the road. As a group they are making that sound, but as the first wave of women walk out of the woods onto the road, the sound suddenly stops. They continue walking, but in total silence. They fill the road and by the hundreds, they keep coming. There is no end to them. And as they pass by us, they do not look our way, but many have one of their hands up, palm facing out, like a greeting or a blessing. Their faces have a seriousness of purpose. As we watch them pass, many of us put our hand up similarly, as a gesture of acknowledgement and respect. Some of us, including me, then put up both hands, palms out, offering supportive energy to them. I feel in the dream that they have come in response to whatever the death or crisis is that has occurred. And I know that their arrival is very important.

Reflections on the dream: This powerful vision shows us the indigenous grandmother's emerging from the woods after holding their secrets for centuries to be revealed at this crucial time on the planet. Now is the time for their secrets and power to be shared with us.

• Celebration
Victoria Hanchin's Dream

I am walking in the woods, and see ahead of me a tree, taller and more magnificent than all the others. I see that there are youths gathered around it, and they have leaned a ladder against the huge trunk. I feel concerned and approach to look into the situation. When I got closer, I see that they are angry adolescent males, climbing up and angrily shaking the branches of this magnificent tree.

I understand that they are angrily shaking the branches, trying to make the tree give them apples. It clearly isn't an apple tree—it's the Tree of Life! They have no idea that they can get so much more from this tree than apples...they can get the Life Force itself! As I understand the situation, the scene of the dream changes.

Now I am witnessing thousands and thousands of women emerging out of the woods, like a flooding river of women, flowing forth—a river of women. I can "zoom-in" to observe particular faces as the women pour forth from the woods.

Watching, I understood that, as women, whether we are ready or not ready, whether we understand or do not understand, whether we have contributed or not contributed, it doesn't matter. It is simply time, and we are all streaming out of the woods in masses of thousands, simply sufficient as we are, responding to the call.

We gather in a huge parking lot bordering the woods, connecting hands in a great circle, as women naturally want to do. But there are too many of us for the parking lot. More and more women are still arriving. The circle we are trying to form cannot be contained by the man-made parking lot.

Then, one of the women opens the circle and begins leading the women single file, all still holding hands, from the circling process, and we come to an adjacent vast, open field. As we arrive in this Great Field, it is set up for us, ready, with thousands of ceremonial masks, painted in red, yellow and blue—the primary colors. The 2-1/2-foot-high masks are propped upright, and adorned with brightly colored, beaded necklaces. These masks and necklaces cover the ground of this enormous Field, and we pour into the Space, each woman taking her place with a mask.

Reflections on the dream: I understand that this field is the "Force and Field of Life" of the Great Mother, the eternal Sacred Feminine, holding the archetypal ancestral collective wisdom of the feminine from all time. This vast Field is an energetic vortex prepared for us from the legacy of ancestral Feminine Power, and it is able to hold all of us, together. All we need to "do" is to be present in the Field, together, in celebration.

I understand that simply showing up en mass, with open hearts, responding to the call, is sufficient to ground and anchor the Mother's Life Force energy, for the birthing of the New Earth. Anything else we do is "icing." The Feminine is sufficiently anchored in to the Earth for the necessary Shift, because we simply show up, responding to the Call.

• Sacred Circle-Net of Light
Beth Blevins' Vision

In the spring of 2007, I had a series of visions of women creating peace. The visions came during individual and group meditation. They unfolded as if I were watching a movie, yet present in them somehow. They were stunningly beautiful, very moving, and sometimes puzzling. In the descriptions and illustrations here, I have attempted to convey the beauty and the power of the scenes that unfolded before my eyes.

The following was one of the first and most powerful for me.

In a Vessels of Peace (VoP) meditation, the facilitator asked us to meditate on the VoP Vessel (see image at the

www.vesselsofpeace.com) and on areas of the world to which we were drawn where women needed support. During the silent meditation that followed, I experienced a vividly detailed, moving vision of peace.

I saw that we were a great, sacred circle of women holding hands in numbers that encircled the entire globe. It was a joining of many sacred circles. The Vessel of Peace stood at the center of the great circle, rising above us and glowing golden white. In unison, all the women in the great circle began walking toward the Vessel, still holding hands. As each woman reached the Vessel, she walked effortlessly through its filigree shell into its core of light. One by one, all merged with it and became the Vessel. We rested in that Oneness, deliciously soaking up the light—the peace, love, and joy contained within it.

In time, we emerged from the Vessel and encircled it once again. We reverently raised our hands to the Heavens in recognition of Divine Oneness and the Sacred Feminine. When we lowered our hands, we found that the edge of a great, weightless net had been placed in them. We already knew what it was and what to do with it. We began walking, walking, spreading out, pulling this great net of peace and healing over the globe. As we pulled the net, some sections of the circle stopped in specific places that needed more intense peace work, and where women were not yet able to join the sacred circle.

Eventually, we all came back together at the opposite side of the globe, having completely encircled Mother Earth with the great net. However, rather than stopping, we continued on back to the Vessel, overlapping our journey and creating a double layer of netting. Again, as we each reached the Vessel, we merged into it. As the last woman merged with the Vessel, however, it shattered! Only golden white light in the shape of the Vessel remained. And this light was us. We were the light.

At once, all of us, as light, leapt into the net! The light began shooting along the cords of the net, streaming through every fiber until the net virtually pulsed with light. Where the cords intersected, the pulsing and the brightness were amplified. And the light was pulsing peace. It was healing Mother Earth.

Slowly, I became aware of the same pulsing filling my body. At first my whole body pulsed, then the pulsing became my heartbeat. And I knew in that moment that my heart was beating in exact unison with each woman in the meditation circle, with every woman in the vision, and with everyone in the world. I remembered that we are truly One.

What is the Stronghold of the Lunar Feminine?

Why is it necessary to address the question of the lunar stronghold?

Let me ask you: Does the earth need oceans? Do hatching eggs need the downy breast of the mother bird and a soft warm nest? Do babies need mother's milk from soft, pillowy breasts? Do we need old growth trees and forests?

I pose these questions to provoke new thoughts and spark conversation. The fact is: the lunar is not being adequately protected. Oceans are being polluted, possibly beyond rectification. Flocks of birds are falling from the skies. Women are mutilating themselves with silicone breast implants in the service of being even more ornamental. Nature is being destroyed for the acquisition of oil.

This is all related to the stronghold of the lunar. We must realize that the lunar feminine is not up to the task of shifting into an appropriate action mode to restore our innate power as women or heal the planet. As an energy, it will not allow the sweeping changes necessary for these changes to happen—at least not without a last effort to maintain the existing model. That is what's happening worldwide right now.

The lunar maintains a stronghold to deny the rising of the solar feminine for many reasons:

- We forgot that power is our birthright and feel lost in how to reclaim it.
- We developed a forced dependency under the 5,000-year patriarchal reign.
- We carry the memories of the burning times in our DNA. This elicits fear, as we begin to step into our power.
- We have few role models of the solar feminine.
- The solar feminine hasn't been activated within us yet. (It just came onto the planet in 2005.)
- Standing up and stepping out can be scary. It can feel dangerous. At times, it is dangerous.
- Change can be difficult, requiring us to make tough decisions.
- We love our circles. They feel good!
- We know and love the lunar. It feels familiar and safe.

Under the 5,000-year period of patriarchal reign, the lunar has been the only face of the feminine available to us. It is human nature to seek safety and survival. But, these are unprecedented times. The safety and survival of the entire planet is at risk.

The lunar is beautiful. She holds tremendous power, the power of Mother Earth, and the Divine Mother. But Mother Earth also demonstrates for us other powers: crashing thunder, bolts of lightning, tsunamis, tornadoes, hurricanes. Mother Earth is more than gentle, receptive, nurturing. We don't know the full extent of how we have affected the weather with our violation of her, but we do know that there is a force of mother nature that is not exclusively lunar.

Floating in beautiful turquoise oceans, snuggling in warm nests, and suckling sweet nectar are all beautiful and these actions raise the vibrations of the planet. However, there will be plenty of time for that once this transition is complete.

What is the Dark Side of the Lunar Feminine?

Just 15 days before the target deadline to complete this manuscript, my editor Charlon and I were incredulous at the energetic stronghold of the shadow aspect of the lunar feminine. We knew it. We felt it. This would not be easy. The lunar did not want to step aside to make room for the solar. Based on what we experienced both individually and in collaboration on this project, we knew the dark side of the lunar feminine was holding on with a death grip.

What was happening? This book was turning into more of a novel or an autobiography of two women engaged in a cosmic battle to open the portal for the power of the solar feminine to be given to women worldwide. The solar is here; her energy is clearly here, but interestingly she is being energetically blocked by women—not men this time, but women—who have internalized the patriarchy so thoroughly that they are fighting to hold onto it.

Damn! Now what? How would we proceed? Charlon headed to the army surplus store to buy combat boots to wear while editing. That was a start. We infused the book with military language. That's another effective strategy. We were determined to keep marching.

Maybe more exploration of how and why this happened would be helpful.

I had a conversation with a friend in her hot tub about the solar feminine and the choice to stay too long in the lunar and to refuse the energy of the solar. I compared our sitting in the ambrosial comfort of the hot tub to marinating in the oxytocin of the lunar feminine. It feels wonderfully warm, safe, comfortable, and nurturing, but we're not meant to stay there forever. This energy is good for a time, but if we stay in too long, the experience can be detrimental.

In trying to make this point, another graphic metaphor comes to mind: puppy mills. My neighbor rescued a dog who was used as a breeder in a puppy mill. She was kept in a cage her entire life, so when she was rescued, her legs were splayed and she couldn't walk. Her function was to provide puppies for the monetary gain of the owners of this obscene machine. The dog survived, but she was debilitated by the system in which she lived.

The lunar has been around for thousands of years. We've learned how to adapt to survive in the machinery of the patriarchy. This includes engaging in countless ways of relinquishing, denying, and hiding our power—even from ourselves. We are so acclimated to it, we don't even know we're doing it, or how to do otherwise. As women in a patriarchal world, our function has been to serve others and to subjugate ourselves. In many ways, it's all we know how to do. There are lots of games we play with ourselves; all the while quietly and obediently squelching our voices, compromising, nurturing, and serving.

What I've discovered is that we have become so acclimated to this—and so debilitated by it—that we cling to this familiarity because we've developed deficits in functioning, just as the breeder dog can't walk because her legs are splayed from spending her life in a cage. We stay in the oxytocin of the hot tub because we don't know how to access our power in a way that allows us to function fearlessly in the world.

The solar feminine carries the powerful energy that is our birthright as women, but we're reluctant to access it because the familiar is so inviting and seems so safe. The dog can no longer run and play. We remain safe and insulated in our circles, in our homes, relying on men to take care of us financially and emotionally.

The new energies of the solar feminine came onto the planet in 2005, in the 11th hour of any hope to reclaim our power and our planet. It's up to us to decide whether we will set aside our denial, defensiveness, and comfort with the familiar, to access the energy that is now available to us to accomplish this important mission.

Now is the time for us to step into our power, remain standing in our power, and march forth together as powerful women in service to the planet.

Why Do Women Remain in the Lunar Feminine?

This is a tough one. I feel like I am going to be received like Bill Cosby when he wrote *Come On People*. In case you missed it, it's a wake up call for African Americans to step into their power.

Alex Haley's powerful book and series *Roots* showed African Americans how their roots were severed and how powerful they were before they were captured and sold into slavery. The female holocaust is not nearly so well documented. Our powerful forgetting keeps us enslaved and the cultural denial of oppression of women discourages us from venturing out.

I admit I didn't read Dr. Cosby's book, but I imagine he is enjoining his people to wake up and remember who they are, just as Alex Haley did.

On the other hand, only a small percentage of women even know about the female holocaust. We usually discover this information in womens' circles or maybe gender studies classes. Eckhart Tolle writes in *The New Earth*, "Nobody knows the exact figure because records were not kept, but it seems certain that during a 300-year-period, between 3 and 5 million women were tortured and killed..."

In my ongoing research on the divine feminine—which is typically the description of the lunar feminine—and my increased awareness of the system of patriarchy, I have come to several realizations.

Women—like African Americans who were forced here on slave boats—have been colonized by the dominant culture. Our roots that contained our powerful connection with Mother Earth were severed during the burning times in Europe. We became emotionally, physically, and spiritually colonized. Colonized people seek safety and security and grow differently than people who have full access to resources, both internal and external. In colonization, people are indoctrinated with powerlessness.

In *Like a Tree*, Jean Shinoda Bolen writes, "When conditions stunt growth, the result is usually a still-recognizable version of a particular kind of tree. In human beings, unless signs of malnutrition or abuse are visible to the eye, the stunted growth that results from withholding love, nutrition, and medical attention, education, and human rights, usually manifests as psychological, intellectual, and spiritual stunting in all concerned."

We have made tremendous progress in women's access to

resources in the West. But there's one primary resource that the patriarchy is still determined not to relinquish: **POWER**. We can pretend we have it when we're sitting in circles with women, but when we step outside those womens' worlds, we subjugate ourselves and quiet our voices to avoid offending the dominant males. We do this because we have internalized a forced helplessness.

In Linda Terry's dream titled *Return of the Indigenous,* she describes this powerful silence she witnessed from the indigenous grandmothers. This silence she heard was a "fierce silence," which is totally different than a "forced silence."

An African American friend said he always admired the Native Americans because they didn't allow themselves to be forced into slavery. This history is not the focus here. What is the focus is the difference between being forced into silence and fiercely, powerfully, choosing silence.

While writing this piece, I was struck at the last sentence and couldn't figure out where to go next. The phone rang and it was a dear friend. I told her I was writing fiercely and was stuck. She offered to help in her powerfully lunar way of loving receptivity. I shared with her that I was writing about my reaction to Linda's dream and her response to the silence. She described the powerful, beautiful silence that evokes truth by connecting with Source. I said, "Yes, I know that silence well. That is the silence that is evoked in meditation, circle process, and essence-to-essence conversations. I told her, "This is not the silence I'm talking about. What I am writing about is the fierce silence that prompted the indigenous people to take their secrets up into the mountains and to hide them from encroaching 'civilization.' This is the fierce silence of secrets kept until it was time for them to be revealed."

This conversation and my powerful internal listening

revealed the awareness that this is what we women have done: we have kept hidden from the dominant culture that we carry enormous power. We have kept it so well hidden that we have even forgotten it ourselves.

In her workshop, *Women Standing In Their Power*, Lucia Rene said that women made an agreement to relinquish our power to give men the experience of experimenting with power.

Barbara Marsiniak, author of *Earth: Pleiadian Keys to the Living Library,* says, "If every women on the planet really knew how much power she had, what do you think the patriarchy would do?"

She writes, "Eons ago, a version of the patriarchy became threatened by female power. So women, in order to hide their power, doubted themselves so men could take a stance and say, "Let's have a chance to run the world and see what it's like." The feminine force took a back seat. Women agreed to believe that they had the curse within their bodies and that (menstrual bleeding) was an indicator of this. Women doubted the very life force within themselves."

Based on our conversation, my dear friend had given me another gift of insight. The reason women remain in the lunar is because that's where we hid our power until it was time to step into it—a circle, a sanctuary, an oxytocin bath, all wonderful places to be until it was the perfect time to collaborate with each other, in our power, actively in the light. Now is the time for us to do this.

We women are like the indigenous who took the secrets into the mountains and caves. Instead, we hid the secrets within ourselves. We have been preparing for this moment in time for thousands of years. We stay too long in the lunar because we still forget how powerful we are and what we came here to do.

I hope this writing activates in you an ancient remembering that you are here to reclaim your severed indigenous roots and reclaim your indigenous soul to reclaim the planet for the Divine Mother

Julie Raymond, author of *We The Trees,* has done extensive research on how we carry these ancient memories in our DNA. It's there; the memories of our indigenous roots, the violence of the severing of these roots, and the 5,000-year occupation by the patriarchy. No wonder it's hard for us to wake up.

As women, we like to nest and nurture. We know how to nest and nurture. But what if the larger nest of the planet, Mother Earth, is being defiled, desecrated, and destroyed? Then, we urgently need to remember who we are, the power we hold, and roar like a mother lion protecting her cubs. We can't continue to allow ourselves to be victimized—the planet to be annihilated—while sitting in circles pretending the lunar is all there is to the feminine. It carries its own power. We need to embody both, but we must activate the solar feminine within us if we are to have a future.

Often I have the mental image of "fiddling while Rome burns." There were people burning in that city! We women are the nurturers, but we need to move beyond living exclusively in the lunar for the sake of our children, our grandchildren, and for the next seven generations.

In *Waking the Global Heart,* Anodea Judith says, "It is not enough to bandage the wounds. We have to stand up and address the slaughter."

We have so much power available to us. It is up to us to recognize and activate this power. This is the energy of the solar feminine. We need to engage it now—powerfully and collaboratively.

Lunar Listening

My deep listening is the space into which this book has expressed itself. To me, deep listening is a primary part of my "original medicine" and an absolutely essential skill for these times, for how else can we work together to resolve the world's current crises? It feels important to share how I came by this practice.

• *My Sacred Wounds*

My initiation into listening began when I was five years old, when I took on the role of confidant for my father. He was a very disturbed man, and after a day of drinking he would pour his pain and misery into me. Intuitively, I knew that my father was dangerous. Intuitively, I was doing my best to keep that violence at bay by being of value to him.

Neither my mother nor my father offered any connection. I was starving. I was desperate. I couldn't allow any of these feelings to surface because they were too overwhelming for me. I did the only thing I could do.

When Dad was vulnerable, I took my entire life force energy and focused it on listening. I listened to Dad as if my life depended on it. He was my only hope and listening was survival, with the energy force of a survival drive. It seemed like a matter of life and death, and it became a way of life.

As I got older, I discovered that being a really good listener was also an opportunity to hide from the world. The outside world I was especially hiding from was my mother who often hit me without provocation. To this day I don't know why. I worked hard to be perfect for her, but when that didn't change anything, I used my listening to become invisible and keep myself safe.

I came to see that if I was listening to other people and

inviting them to share their stories, I didn't have to express myself. And in not expressing myself, I was safe from the reactions of others. Listening became my strategy for protecting myself from the outside world.

So my practice in deep listening had its roots in real life experiences, in what I now call my sacred wounds. I listened to my parents' dysfunctions, becoming absorbed in them, losing myself and my feelings to their pain, their risks, their experiences.

• *Love is Present*

My childhood also contained the roots of my healing. My grandfather died when I was five years old. For me, not only had he been extraordinarily safe, but also extraordinarily loving. I basked in his love, which became like a seed inside me. When my grandfather died, I had only my father. And I knew my father was dangerous for me.

So I did a funny thing in my mind. I put my grandfather's face on my father, so that I could love him. It was safe then to love my father because I had made him into my grandfather. Despite the fact that my father's behavior fluctuated wildly, the loving energy connected to my relationship with my grandfather came to be associated with the listening energy.

I learned how to love, and how to be loved from my grandfather. I associated my grandfather with my father so I could see him as I saw my grandfather, rather than as the way he was, and love him. As I learned to listen to my father, I created a connection in my mind between listening and loving.

• *The Gift Matures*

I've worked on myself diligently for the past 32 years—in therapy since I was thirty—to discover the essence of what I know from these experiences. With therapy, education, and spiritual understanding, the listening that kept me alive as a child is now a finely-crafted art form. My survival strategy has become the foundation of a gift I offer others; the way of life I learned in response to my childhood wounds has become a safe container in which others can come to know about themselves.

I'm a successful psychotherapist. I am a master of love-listening, offering a safe stage for my clients to express the deepest aspects of themselves and heal their deepest wounds. This kind of listening requires a still mind that does not judge or react, and a heart that is open and loving.

When I listen this way, people are incredibly interesting. I'm fascinated with their inner workings—the brilliance of the unconscious. How do our experiences cause us to make certain decisions? I wonder.

People ask me, "Don't you get burned out?" or "Don't you feel burdened?" Honestly, I don't. I get tired because my brain is working, but every person that walks through my office door, every session, every time they come in, it's an entirely new experience.

I don't know what they're going to discover. I don't know what I'm going to discover. I don't know what pieces of the puzzle might reveal themselves in that particular session. It's continually intriguing to me.

Part of what I do is to use my love-listening space to extend loving energy and witness energy to the person who's sitting across from me. I think it was my study of *The Course in Miracles* that most matured this ability. For a number of years and in many workbook exercises, I learned about extending love. And I had a lot of experience with the power of that loving energy, that higher vibration, becoming confident in that power. I developed a felt sense of extending love which is a joyous feeling inside. So, it's a mutual blessing for me to extend love. Because my therapeutic container—my office—is so often filled with this energy of love-listening-extended, I experience my office as a temple.

• Listening Within and Becoming Visible

Naturally, as a psychotherapist I'm also paying attention to what comes up within me—what my guidance or intuition reveals. Learning to listen to my own inner voice was an essential part of healing and maturing my gift. And as I learned the lesson, I came out of hiding, listened to, and expressed my own understandings and realizations. I built my capacity to create a field of listening/loving not only for other people, but also for myself.

And as I've understood and freed my gift, I've been increasingly drawn to share it; it's time for me to step out onto the stage of my life. My willingness, comfort, and desire to be visible grow exponentially. I am ready to be visible, not only to myself, but to others.

This moment is a big turning point for me. In the past, I've been committed to being invisible, very committed, survival-committed. My willingness to take the stage now is not only the outcome of my therapeutic and spiritual processes, but also because of how valuable deep listening is for these times.

As a psychotherapist, I create the stage for someone else. Now I find myself wanting to be a successful public speaker—which is the ultimate visibility—because what I have to contribute, my knowledge, is important. I've become so effective at listening to my inner voice and hearing the intelligence that comes from within me, I can just stand on a stage or sit in a circle and let it come through me. Then, I'm a conduit and it's magical.

Prior to my therapy, I never felt entitled to have anyone listen to me. But for the past 5-10 years I've worked diligently on this visibility piece. It's clearly time to share what I've learned, for my own growth, but also because it is an offering that will help heal the divisiveness that is so prevalent today. What I've learned from my sacred wounds—skills of deep love listening, listening to others, listening to myself, teaching others to listen to themselves—is essential information for these times.

Listening as the New Weaponry

In the first phases of creating the energetic vortex of *Women Waking the World,* I met with my three co-creators in Northern California—the location chosen strategically and specifically because of its powerful vortex.

As part of our process, each of us asked for guidance about the particular gifts (original medicine) that we brought to the project. When my "sister" Vikki focused on me, what surfaced was a concept of listening as the new weaponry. Vikki is a staunchly nonviolent person and was baffled by the word weaponry. At first, she struggled against this word. Ultimately, however, she acquiesced, allowing the word that kept coming into her deep inner listening state.

Several weeks later, after much conversation, Vikki agreed to ask for guidance on the word weaponry, as we are all committed to nonviolence. The response is included in its entirety on the following pages.

Listening As the New Weaponry

© Divine Wisdom received by
Victoria Hanchin 7/4/2009

I AM Mother Durga. I come in the service of Divine Truth and Divine Wholeness.

I AM She who was invoked in ancient days to save the Earth, when all the masculine weaponry failed, insufficient and ineffective in vanquishing the greed demon destroying the Earth who even the gods could not defeat.

I, Mother Durga, emerged then, radiant with my Feminine Presence and power, laughing. I easily vanquished that destructive consciousness, fearsome and disempowering, that threatened all life.

Such is the time we are again facing on our beloved Earth. Again there is a demon of greed consciousness on Earth. And I, Durga, am returning again to vanquish that force which cannot be destroyed by man or gods—because it was created by this same masculine-polarized consciousness of separation and domination, out of balance with the feminine. And because of this extreme imbalance, a Feminine power from a different consciousness is the only hope.

I am returning. I am returning within that feminine place of the heart. I am arising this time within the hearts of those who must encounter these current demons of greed, separation, and domination.

Once again we engage in an epic battle, on the sorrowful battlefield of duality: those whose polarizing and embattling ways dismantle, harm and destroy Life, countering those whose ways nourish, sustain, and transform Life.

When I was invoked to save the Earth before, I vanquished the demon, outwitting him in his own forms of battle. Now with the current forms of destruction terrorizing Earth, I introduce a new form of encounter on the polarized battlefield of duality: Reciprocal Listening.

I, Durga, bring forward Listening as the new weaponry. And I will have many in my ranks. This weaponry of reciprocal listening disarms the consciousness of separation and polarization, the extreme form of which is violence and war.

This new weaponry is a form of listening that is governed by the heart and not the head. This form of listening seeks not to dominate, judge or defeat, but to unify. Because this form of listening seeks to receive, to understand, to forgive, to restore respect and right relationship, it has the power to unify opposites.

This new weaponry of Reciprocal Listening holds the miracle of unifying the masculine and the feminine, first unifying them inwardly and then outwardly in such a way that neither dominates the other, but instead they are held in balance. It is like the miracle of fire and water, where the fire does not vaporize the water, and the water does not douse the fire.

Now this new Listening weaponry will be massively deployed on a global basis, as never before. This new weaponry brings the polarized elements together in deeply engaged and receptive relatedness, through profound heart-opening listening. This reciprocal listening, through words of truth and beyond words, allows an energetic merging of hearts and recognition of oneness. This is not just a weaponry of women. We will have ranks of heart-activated men who will train other men in this new weaponry of unification. There are many who are already eager to enlist and to serve. Gratitude, unity, and harmony will be the spoils of this battlefield.

> "*I have an assignment to play*
> *a huge role in helping women*
> *wake up on the planet.*"
> – NENIE BEANIE

The Conversation that Opened the Door

"The Circle of Love is never broken," my sister Nene said, her last words before she slipped into a non-responsive state and left her body at 11:11 AM, Friday, August 13, 2004. Four days after her death, Nene began communicating with me. And for the past 6 years, our love has been the channel for an amazing conversation across the veil. This book is written in collaboration with Nene.

In the winter of 1989, Nene was diagnosed with 4th stage metastasized breast cancer, and given a probability of 6 months to live. She had 6-month-old twins—Robert and Katlyn, and a son Josh. She was a single mother of three. Her response was complete surrender. Her words were, "Not my will, but Thy will; whatever is best for the children." Evidently, what was best for the children is that she live 14 more years.

During those 14 years she focused passionately on nourishing her soul and releasing her ego. As time passed, it was clear that her "marching orders" were to become the most powerful spiritual being possible in preparation for her death—her transition—which was always "just on the other side of the door."

Three days after Nene transitioned, a curious set of happenings caught my attention as I made my way to work. I came to a stop sign, and as I waited to move into another lane, a car drove up next to me. As it pulled ahead, too late to wave, I saw that it was my sister Cathy.

When I arrived at my office building and put my hand on the doorknob, it turned in my hand. I found myself stepping back to let someone walk out the door. No one was there.

I climbed the stairs approaching my suite of offices. Once again, as I put my hand on the doorknob, someone turned the knob from the other side. Once again, I stepped back to allow them to walk through. No one. At this point I exclaimed out loud, "What's going on with doors?"

I proceeded to my office, sat down, and began attending to my first client of the day. As I opened my listening space, a clear voice in my head stated, "I'm just on the other side of the door." This began my ongoing communication with Nene.

Adept at inner listening, it seemed natural to dialogue with Nene this way. I'd connected deeply with myself for so many years, that my felt sense of the subtleties of internal listening allowed me to "hear" Nene's voice distinct from my own thoughts.

I recalled several experiments I'd done years before in automatic writing as a way to connect with my grandfather who died when I was young. I was amazed at the results of asking a question in writing and intuitively listening for the answer. I use this same tool to facilitate my ongoing conversations with Nene.

• Sparks From My Sister

The Solar Sparks sprinkled throughout this book are Nene's (Nenie Beanie's) insights about the energy of the solar feminine. These words carry an energy that comes from a higher dimension and will infuse you with the unique vibration of that dimension.

> "The present moment is the point from which power erupts."
> — NENIE BEANIE

2

Transition

As the earth is in transition, midwifed by women, so too
are we women in transition. From our deep connection with
the lunar, to igniting and embodying the solar feminine,
ultimately we will achieve a magnificent balance of the
lunar and solar within.

Anyone who has given birth or witnessed it knows that
transition is messy and difficult. We fear what is new,
clinging desperately to what is comfortable and familiar,
hovering in the vastness between what was and what is.
With no solid support beneath our feet, transition is an
especially challenging time because our cells carry the
memories of the consequences for standing in our power.
Ramifications have been dire for thousands of years—up to,
and including, today.

As we come together, welcoming one another into the
solar—not attempting to pull each other back out of fear—
we will do what we came to do. With our willingness to be
an active part of this transition process; the receptive,
welcoming, inclusive energy of the lunar will welcome and
embrace the solar feminine.

Heightened Awareness as a Tool for Transition

As mentioned in the introduction, in the spring of 2010 I discovered Lucia Rene, author of *Unplugging the Patriarchy*. Her message and actions were so powerful and I connected so strongly with her that I invited her to conduct a workshop in my city.

Three of the aspects of Lucia's work that attracted me were her comfort with the word "patriarchy;" her description of the solar feminine; and ironically, her use of military language.

I never imagined I would be making a case for the use of military language. As I questioned and explored this attraction to the use of these words, I've learned a great deal. The first thing I discovered is that this language inspires power and action. The second aspects I discovered were precision and single focus. A third crucial quality of military language is the energy of strategizing groups or troops, and acting in unison or collaboration. These are all qualities that are absent in the lunar feminine.

As I shared previously, I encountered a distinct conflict between the energies of the lunar feminine—receptivity, nurturing, inclusiveness, and deep listening—and the solar feminine. The lunar in women is universally accepted in the patriarchal culture.

The solar feminine, on the other hand, is an entirely different set of traits. It includes standing in one's own power, taking action, navigating the world effectively, and living without apology. These aspects are clearly rejected, within women, by both genders in the patriarchal culture.

My role is to activate and ignite the role of the collective feminine in planetary awakening. As a writer and speaker on this topic, I am strongly moved by the energy of "mother bear fierceness." The energy of the lunar feminine has its place and it's an important one, but at this unprecedented time on the planet, the lunar feminine is not up to the task of reversing the trajectory the planet has been on under patriarchy for the last 5,000 years.

Now is the time for the solar feminine to come out of the shadows, move into the light, stand in her power collaboratively with her sisters, and march forward strategically in the service of the Divine Mother and Mother Earth.

Lunar as the Fertile Soil

As I focus on the energy of the solar feminine, it is crucial that this powerful energy field not be misinterpreted as women just acting like domineering men. To flourish, the solar feminine must be grounded in the lunar energies of receptivity, expansiveness, and unconditional love.

I'm only beginning to understand the powerful balance of lunar and solar within, that creates a dynamic synergy. It is effective for each of us to embody both and oscillate between the two within ourselves and each other.

An example of moving back and forth within might be spending time in meditation and then taking action from guidance. Moving from lunar to solar between women might look like listening deeply to another while she speaks powerfully about her passions or experiences.

The lunar without the solar and the solar without the lunar are significantly less effective. It is so clear that at this pivotal time on the planet, effectiveness and efficiency is imperative.

Think of the lunar as the womb, or the fertile soil, from which the solar can spring forth. Much like a garden plot, well-composted and well-tilled is the ground from which a powerful, healthy, strong plant bursts forth. The lunar is the soil and the solar is the plant.

The necessity of going inward and exploring is the focus of my book, *Mining for Diamonds*. I end it by writing, "We live in a world that focuses on the external...material things; esteem from others; and, of course, money. Many people don't even think in terms of an inner world... feelings, thoughts, and values. In fact, this inner world is where true wealth resides."

The inner world is the ground of being from which action comes. It was in this exploration and comfort with my inner world that I came to connect with Nene. This consistent practice of inner listening yielded a rock solid trust in my own inner knowing.

Holding space, listening deeply with unconditional love are powerful ways the lunar supports the solar.

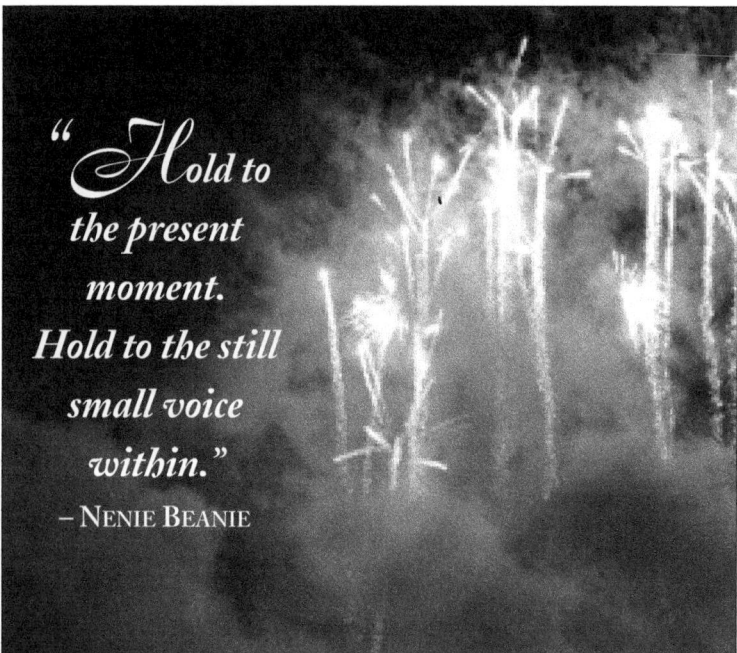

"*Hold to the present moment. Hold to the still small voice within.*"
– NENIE BEANIE

What is the Role of Men During the Solar Feminine Awakening?

When I speak about the role of the collective feminine in planetary awakening, I am frequently met with the question, "What about the men?" Occasionally, someone will ask, "Doesn't this make me a man hater?" There are many answers to these questions, and it is important to address them so we're not caught in defensiveness and justification.

One of my favorite writers, Llewellyn Vaughn-Lee writes in his book, *The Return of the Feminine and the World Soul:*

"The light of the soul of the world needs the participation of all who are open to this work. But part of our redemption of the feminine is to acknowledge that certain work can only be done by women. The interconnections of life belong to the wisdom of the feminine, and a woman's body holds the knowledge of how the world interrelates.

"Masculine consciousness imaged a transcendent divinity—the feminine knows how the divine is present in every cell of creation. Women know this not as abstract knowledge but part of their instinctual nature—in the womb the light of a soul can come into physical form. Life is standing at the edge of an abyss of forcefulness waiting for the light of the world to be born. This birth needs the wisdom of the feminine and women must take their place in this time of great potential."

Numerous sources reveal that the staff of power is being handed to the feminine in 2012; evidence is everywhere. There are more female heads-of-state than ever before, and women are moving into positions of leadership at every level. When the system allows, they often lead in a new way that is inclusive, expansive, creative, and vulnerable. Aligned with their feminine qualities, women naturally invite others to grow and expand, understand and practice the sanctity of life, and function from a well of creativity and love.

This is not a power shift against men in any way. This is the true power that grows grass through cracks in cement. It recognizes and affirms life, and its deep interconnections call for behavior that serves all life.

In this energetic environment calling women to rise in this powerful and crucial way, what then is the role of men? According to Vaughn-Lee, men are called now, "To protect women in this work; to value, honor, and consciously protect the work being done by women, not to allow any interference in the process. This is the role of the masculine as the protector."

He continues, "How this role will be expressed is difficult to say. Perhaps, there will be as many expressions as there are men who see the need. There are so many negative forces in the world that don't want this work to be done, that don't want the world's citizens to awaken, and that oppose having women regain their power. This is threatening to the power structures that we live under because womens' power is decentralized, self-organizing, and not controllable because it is life-force itself."

In the last chapter of this book, Lucia Rene tells us that men's reactions to women regaining their power is a necessary step, just as women stepping forward now is a necessary step. Women assuming their rightful roles will build the fuel necessary to open mens' hearts, just as women must open their power centers now.

Ultimately, we are each called to find the feminine life force and masculine protector within ourselves. We must become conscious and involved in a balanced way, both feminine and masculine. The women's movement opened the door for women to take on more traditionally masculine qualities like initiative, roles outside the home, and a more assertive energy. In a way, women are moving more quickly now than men to balance their masculine and feminine qualities. The current spirituality movement toward heart-centered thought and action will be a vehicle for men to begin activating their more lunar qualities.

As we move more toward increased awareness of our spiritual aspects, our gender identities will become less significant. Our right and left brains will find their correct balance within both men and women. From the work of Teilhard De Chardin, we will all move from being "human beings having a spiritual experience, to spiritual beings having a human experience."

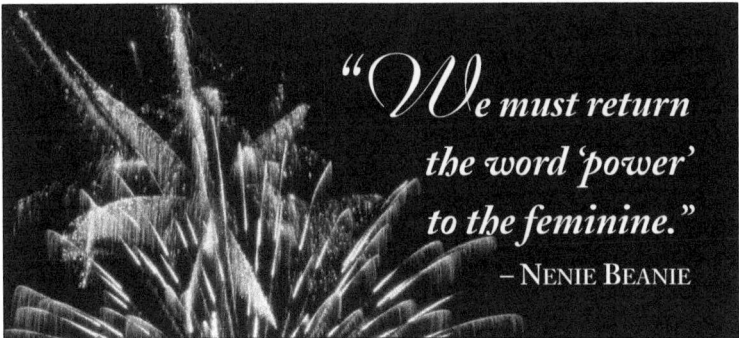

> *"We must return the word 'power' to the feminine."*
> – NENIE BEANIE

Solar Feminine / Lunar Masculine

Is solar feminine just another term for a woman acting like a man?

During one of my daily walks in the woods with my friend Kathy and our dogs, Noche and Daisy, she posed an important question. She asked, "Why do women in power often model the worst aspects of men?" She continued,

"Why are so many strong women aggressive, domineering, and bossy?"

I believe the answers to these questions are complicated by the dominant culture and certainly, corporate social norms. This observation provides an opportunity to differentiate between the solar feminine and a woman acting like a man.

The solar feminine embodies energies of strength, action, creativity, and being strongly connected with the lower three chakras.

1. Chakra 1: The root chakra, associated with red, is connected with being grounded in the earth.

2. Chakra 2: The sacral chakra, associated with orange, is associated with creativity and sexuality.

3. Chakra 3: The solar plexus chakra, associated with yellow, is connected to power and will.

The solar feminine is related to activation and alignment with these three energy centers. As you can see, there is nothing here that conveys aggression, manipulation, dominance, or control over others. Standing in power is standing in our own power, not trampling or usurping the power of others.

Celia Fenn writes, "The solar feminine began coming onto the planet in 2005." Until then we had few effective models, or even energetic support for being a woman in power. Acting like men may have been our only option, especially in corporate settings. Now we do have a much more effective, natural choice available to us.

The lunar masculine, as well, is different than a man who simply takes on the more negative feminine qualities such as passivity, ineffectiveness, lack of initiative, and dependence. Celia Fenn says, "The lunar masculine is gentle, nurturing, and caring." Many teachers tell us that it is time for men to move into their hearts. This powerful heart energy has been denied to men during this 5,000-year patriarchal era. The head, or intellect, has been welcomed and honored, while the heart has been completely denied. It is time for men to move into their hearts. Our planetary future requires it.

Men and women, both balanced and grounded in their lunar and solar aspects, is the direction in which we are headed. This is much more healthy than both genders functioning with a limited skill set and depending on the other gender for balance.

Finding Balance by Marching in Circles

All this talk about the lunar and solar feminine smacks of wholeness and balance. If I'm writing a book to put the solar feminine on the map, why do I keep going back to the lunar?

The answer to that question is multi-faceted. It sets my head to spinning. There are so many aspects to this that I'm going to begin by moving into a free association mode and write whatever pops up.

"What is valuable to understand about the ideal balance between the lunar and the solar?"

1. The lunar has been here for thousands of years. As women, we access this readily.

2. The solar only showed up on the planet in 2005. Most of us are only beginning to know about it and embody it.

3. Because we're unfamiliar with the solar, we habitually move into the lunar default mode.

4. The planet is in dire straights and passionate, powerful, effective action is imperative.

5. The lunar holds the space and the solar takes the action.

6. The solar embodies the activation of the lower three chakras which includes being deeply connected and grounded in Mother Earth, passion and creativity, and a strong sense of personal power.

7. Some teachers tell us that now is the time to pass the baton of powerful heart activation to the men. Living from the heart is something women have mastered. It is now time for men to be centered there.

8. These same teachers have discovered that power is the natural birthright of women, which we relinquished under patriarchy.

9. Access to the heart was relinquished by men under patriarchy.

This section was originally titled, "Circles and Teams." What does all this have to do with circles and teams?

Early in the book-writing process I repeatedly came across the phrase "circles and teams"—such contrasting concepts! Also, the phrase "Marching in Circles" surfaced over and over again.

Circles

1. Circles have tremendous value. They create and hold extraordinary power. Wisdom is spoken into–and invited by–circle energy.

2. Women who have been invisible under patriarchy see one another into visibility and hear each other into our voices in the circle process.

3. Circles embody unconditional love and acceptance. Circles nurture. Women deeply connect with each other in circles.

Teams

1. Inherent in teams is the unified action toward one goal.

2. Team members work together and channel resources and support to the team member who has the best potential for reaching the goal.

3. Teams strategize. They create plans of action to realize their mutual goals.

4. They practice together and alone. They remain focused on their goals.

Fascinating contrast between circles and teams, but can they come together?

Now, let's explore "Marching in Circles." What can this mean?

Marching

Marching is a single-pointed forward movement, usually performed in unison, by a group of people with a common goal. That's clear enough.

Circle

A circle is around something, maybe even an empty space with no clear beginning or end. We all feel that a circle is a powerful symbol. The last words my sister, Nene, spoke before she died were, "The circle of love is never broken."

We know circles are powerful, as is marching, but how do they fit together? At this point, I have a few clues:

1. The planet is round.

2. Do we march forth in circles? Do we take the wisdom and unconditional love from the circle process and carry these qualities into the march?

3. Both circles and marching embody unity.

In bringing these ideas together...

Men hold us in their hearts (the circle of love) as we march forth in powerful unified action and focus as a "nation of women."

Llewellyn Vaughan-Lee writes, "The role of men is to protect women in this work—to value it and to consciously protect it. This is the role of the masculine as protector; that you (men) honor this work that is being done by women and you don't allow it to be interfered with. How will that get played out I don't know. There are so many negative forces in the world that don't want this work to be done that don't want the world to be activated again, and that oppose having the women regain their power because women's power is decentralized, it is organic, it cannot be manipulated, it cannot be controlled—it is life."

Vaughan-Lee states in this quote, "How will that get played out I don't know." A powerful awareness arises in me in response to that question. It gets played out by men moving into their hearts on a global scale.

We think of men as protectors, but especially under patriarchy, 99.9% of the destruction and harm to us and the rest of the planet has been done by men. The two-fold process of moving out of this dominator, destroyer mode of being and moving into the heart serves the purpose of protecting us AND propelling us forward in a circle of love!

So, Marching in Circles is marching forth, enveloped in the love of the men of heart who hold us in the circle of love. Wow!

" *You are a choicemaker. Every choice you make has a result.*"
— NENIE BEANIE

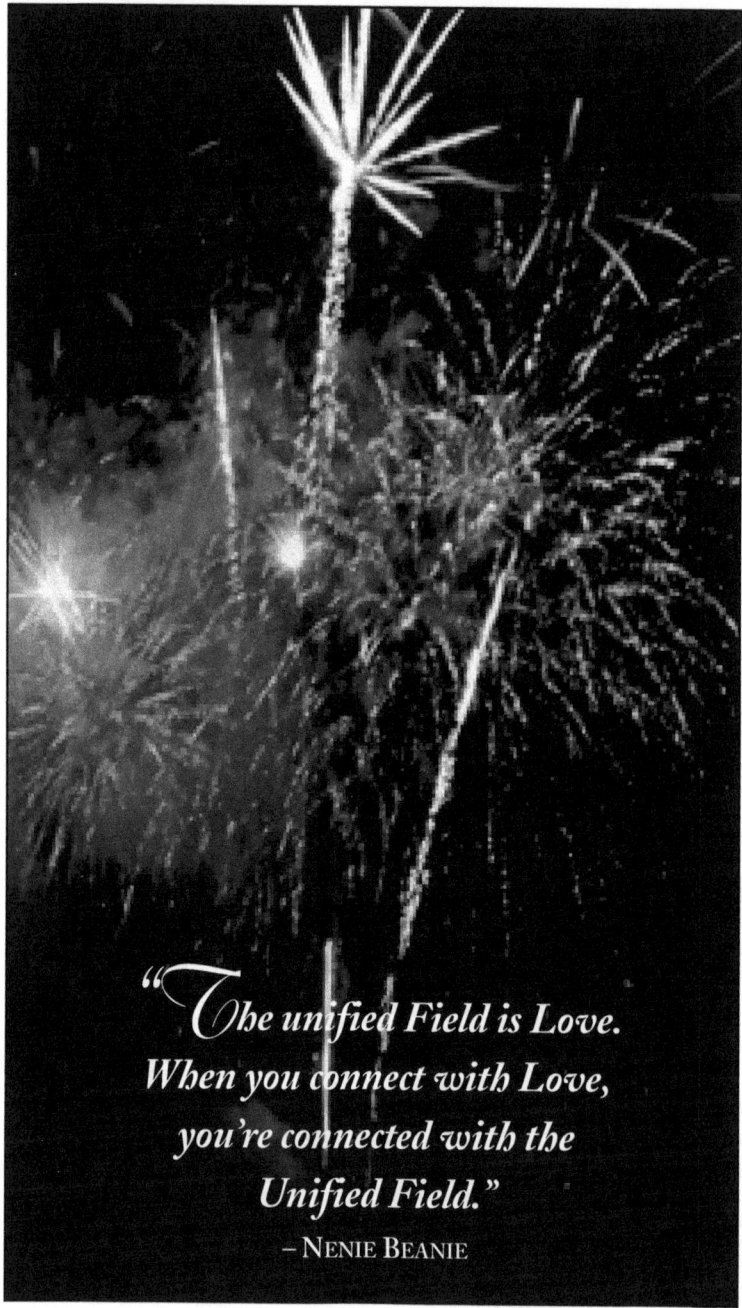

*"The unified Field is Love.
When you connect with Love,
you're connected with the
Unified Field."*
— NENIE BEANIE

3

First Glimpses of Dawn

As I walked with my friend at the exact moment of the vernal equinox, we trudged through the sleet, ice pellets pounding our faces. She spread her arms and exclaimed, "Now, it's Spring. The flowers will pop open, the sun will break through and the trees will explode into new life any minute now." We laughed because her comment and our Spring visions were in stark contrast to the grey sky, icy rain, and bone-chilling wind. We still knew, though, that Spring had arrived and the promise of its coming gave us hope.

Just as we can feel the murmurings of Spring even though she hasn't fully shown up, we can also feel the emergence of dawn while it is still dark. We trust that day follows night and Spring follows Winter as it has for eons.

These are dark times. It feels as if the darkness is fighting the Light. Lucia Rene used the metaphor of an animal cornered into a crevice, fighting for its life. The dark forces hold on with a death grip. We must remember and have faith in the arrival of dawn—the arrival of Spring. We are here, now.

The solar feminine is being ignited—activated, just as the sun begins to rise in the sky and shed new light onto the earth. The early Spring energy offers its life force to the newly emerging shoots and buds.

As women, we embrace and welcome the solar feminine as she arrives on the planet to provide the needed push to usher in the New Age, as we experience the death throes of the old world.

As dawn arrives, the night recedes.

Dawn

Spring is an especially vibrant time of year. Everything seems fresh, and there's an energy of anticipation and excitement. Similar new beginnings cross my mind: babies, weddings, puppies, new green peeking up through the snow, and mud. Spring emanates hope in the midst of the cold and dark.

I often liken Spring to the dawn of the feminine on the planet. Many prophecies tell us that this is the beginning of a 13,000-year period of moving toward—and realizing—a New Earth. Is there a more awesome beginning imaginable? Those of us who showed up at this time chose to be here to witness, experience, and facilitate the beginning of a New Age.

We have all slept through dawn, probably more often than not. We have sleep-walked through Spring as well. What a gift to ourselves to not sleep through this greatest beginning of all time.

I vividly remember a story Marianne Williamson told about her experience with dawn. When she lived in Michigan, her bedroom window was positioned such that she awoke at the first morning light every morning and was awestruck by the beauty of dawn. She described it in a way that activated within me my already strong feelings about dawn.

When I wrote *What Happens When Women Wake Up?* I also wrote a piece about dawn that I wanted to use in the book. I worked and worked with this writing and solicited huge amounts of editing support to no avail. I was not able to include it in the book. In retrospect, I now realize that I was attempting to force something that wasn't ready yet. I wanted to announce the dawn of the collective feminine on the planet through the metaphor of dawn. It didn't work. It couldn't work. It wasn't time.

At the beginning of 2011, I spoke with Lucia Rene. She asked me if I wanted to know the difference between 2010 and 2011. Of course I said, "Yes." She responded, "In 2010, women were coming onto the scene in large numbers and now in 2011 we are fully in the light, center stage."

My promptings to herald the dawn of the collective feminine on the planet were accurate, but a little premature. Now, as I revisit the energy of dawn for this new book, it is with an additional perspective that could come only with the passage of time and certain events that had to occur first, the most important of these being my introduction to the energies of the solar feminine. I now see that the dawn of the collective feminine MUST include this crucial aspect of the feminine.

The lunar feminine is beautiful, but it is not equipped to carry the staff of power alone. It is the newer energies of the solar feminine that usher in the dawn of the New Earth.

> "*Trust yourself; listen to yourself; use your voice; stand in your power.*"
> — NENIE BEANIE

Solar Feminine Power

Power is a maligned word. We tend to automatically connect the word power with "abuse of power." Under the patriarchal paradigm—the dominator model of society—this is a common association. But wielding power over others is a violation, not true power, and we are now living through a shift in how power is held. Womens' power is key.

Vikki Hanchin writes in her powerful booklet, *Awakening Women: Igniting Global Transformation,* that this transfer of power has been predicted by Mayan teachings. The final glyph of the Dresden Kodah shows the staff of power being handed to the feminine at the onset of the New Age, December 21, 2012.

Feminine power is not a power over, but power with. Collaboration is the basis of the new expression of power, resulting in a feminine leadership style that acknowledges vulnerability and offers support and deep reciprocal listening. This style leads to a feeling of connection, rather than competition, which moves us closer to Oneness and community.

Anodea Judith's book, *Waking the Global Heart,* documents humanity's rite of passage from the love of power to the power of love. Teilhard de Chardin said, "Someday, after mastering the winds, the waves, the tides and gravity, we shall harness for God the energies of love, and then, for a second time in the history of the world, man will have discovered fire." Because women tend to be more heart-centered, we are the appropriate gender to usher in this new age with the power of love, nurturance, collaboration, and "mother bear fierceness."

This fierce quality of love with which a mother bear protects her cubs is more and more necessary as the atrocities against Mother Earth, women, children, and animals continue. And rightfully so. The British Petroleum oil volcano—which destroyed life in an unprecedented way—activated this "mother bear fierceness in countless women." Lucia Rene said of this obscene act of violation, greed and exploitation, "They crossed the line." Thousands of women felt the pain in their own bellies, and tears ran down their cheeks as they felt in themselves this rape of Mother Earth.

According to Lucia, the power of heart-centered love is to be coupled with the third chakra power of the collective feminine saying with every fiber of our beings, "Enough is enough." Under patriarchy womens' right to say, "No," was denied. Now at this unprecedented time in humanity's history, we shout out with a resounding, "No," to the forces that are set on exploiting and defiling our precious Earth. Mother's love must include an emphatic "No" to safeguard against further damage.

To turn this ship around, the power of love must be applied firmly and collectively, with each woman standing in the power of herself, willing to say, "Enough is enough."

• *Tend and Befriend*

The male principle includes independence, autonomy, risk-taking, the hero's journey, and going it alone. The feminine principle is almost the polar opposite. It includes bonding, nurturing, caretaking, and connecting. Power for women and men is entirely different.

When their survival is threatened, men respond with a flight or fight response, each individual standing for their own survival. In many ways, this is a physiological system that supports individual power.

When the survival of women is threatened, they respond

with a tend and befriend response with an oxytocin release, which evokes behaviors such as reaching out, connecting, and nurturing. This is a physiological system that supports the power of connection.

The power of connection is the kind of power that is necessary now. More individual power at cross-purposes will only make the crises on the planet more extreme. Now is the time to access feminine power on a planetary scale. Our survival as a species is being threatened. We must tend and befriend each other worldwide to buttress this evolutionary leap.

"It's crucial for us to collaborate with one another with the greatest power we can access."

– NENIE BEANIE

4

Stealing Onto the Planet

Now, she's here, the solar feminine, no longer a hint or a whisper, but standing fully, powerfully, in the light of day.

However, she comes with a little commotion. Just as a seed cracks open to become a sprout and break through the soil, there is discomfort; some might even perceive it as violent. The fact is: the throes of birth are noisy and violent.

Exploring the energies of anger—and the power of anger channeled in the service of life—is a crucial piece of the emergence of this dramatic energy.

Inherent in the energy of the solar feminine is action. Using the power and energy of anger in service to the planet and Her people is a controversial topic among men and women, but one that can no longer be ignored.

Of all the content in this book, I know the writings about anger have the potential to elicit the most reaction and resistance. That is okay. Have your reaction. Allow your resistance if that's what comes up for you. But also recognize that the source of your reaction or resistance may be a natural reaction to change, BIG change; even linked to maintaining the status quo.

It is my sacred duty to deliver this message—period—without white-washing it, diluting it, or changing it in an effort to make it pleasant. Change never feels natural, but neither does patriarchy. As time passes, the myriad structures of patriarchy become even less tolerable. I have my marching orders and am committed to delivering this message in its purest form.

If not now, I welcome you to join this movement of action, spurred by anger, when you are inspired. If you are ready now, read on.

Anger as a Powerful Catalyst for Positive Change

Anger is the hardest emotion for women to manage.

I love sharing the story my daughter-in-law, Jen, shared with me.

When my granddaughter Livvie was an infant, sleeping peacefully, all of a sudden she would wake and absolutely RAGE. Jen nursed and soothed her, and rocked her to sleep. Sometime later, Livvie would wake and rage again. Jen found this behavior fascinating. I love the story because it shows us how honestly we come by rage. We're born with it. It's not good or bad; it's natural.

Because this is such an important topic for women, here are two more stories.

The next story is about a 4-year-old boy who was mute for emotional reasons and in a program for emotionally impaired children. During a staff meeting, one psychiatrist announced that the little boy walked up to him and said, "I hate you." The other psychiatrist smiled and said to him, "What an honor it is that he chose to share his anger with you."

An additional story about anger is about Jonathon Swift. In line to become the Archbishop of Canterbury, this position meant more than anything else to him. He fully expected to receive the assignment. For political reasons, it was not offered to him. He was enraged. The action he chose—fueled by his anger—was to pen *Gulliver's Travels*.

Three interesting stories; three important lessons about anger:

1. It is natural.
2. It is a gift.
3. It motivates action.

Now, what is the value of denying and suppressing anger? It is an energy; it does exist, but unfortunately, we women are socially programmed to deny it, direct it inward, or as Marianne Williamson says, "pour pink paint over it." What if anger was acknowledged, honored, embraced, and used to channel powerful action?

This is pretty scary stuff. After all, none of us wants to be called a bitch, or referred to as "an angry woman." We will avoid it at all costs, compromising our very selves in the process. Sweet, nice, passive, apologetic, yielding, no muss no fuss; these qualities are oh so familiar, as we obediently maintain the status quo. But then again, the status quo appears to be on a trajectory toward the destruction of us all. But, for God's sake, don't get mad!

We women are so nice that we've been known to apologize to chairs when bumping into them or silencing our voices in the face of true injustice. "Stepping into our power" means owning our anger without apology.

Anger is real, anger is valid, and anger is often 100% justified when we allow ourselves to attune ourselves to the pure emotion of it and express from that power-place. Owning anger; claiming anger; feeling anger; using anger to fuel our actions in the service of the planet; now, there's a force to be reckoned with!

Let me be clear: the anger of which I speak is not indiscriminate or destructive. I'm talking about the ability to simply identify within ourselves when we're angry and express it in a constructive manner, rather than suppressing it and turning it inward to manifest in damaging ways, e.g., depression and eating disorders.

Mother Earth and all her inhabitants require that women step into our power collaboratively, in the service of all life. Remaining quiet, nice little girls who offend no one is not of value at this unprecedented time on the planet.

• *MADD Mothers*

Most of us know about a very powerful group of very angry women. These women have saved thousands of lives by using their anger constructively. They are so effective that almost everyone knows who they are. Their acronym is MADD; Mother's Against Drunk Driving.

In my small hometown 35 years ago, there was a teenager who killed two people, on two separate occasions, by drunk driving. It was a rumor, and maybe even a scandal, but he experienced no repercussions from the court system. Three-and-a-half decades later, nationally we all know that drinking and driving has dire consequences. Countless lives have been saved by this group of very angry women.

It's easy to justify their anger because their children were killed. But what would happen if we expanded our circle of anger-in-action to include the entire planet, the animals, the water, the trees, and the skies?

Is a mother bear angry when she protects her young? She's simply operating on instinct, willing to do anything and everything to preserve the life of her cubs. Are women angry who stand up powerfully and collaboratively in the service of all life? They're simply operating on instinct, willing to do anything and everything to preserve the life of the planet.

While it's true that anger can be used to hurt others, anger can also be used in the same constructive, effective way the women of MADD have saved countless lives.

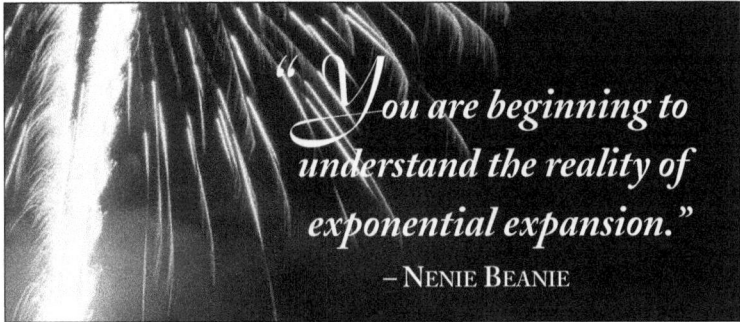

> *"You are beginning to understand the reality of exponential expansion."*
> — NENIE BEANIE

• *Reclaiming Our Power Through Anger*

Llewellyn Vaughan-Lee says, "To fully encounter the divine feminine—the creative principle of life—we must be prepared for her anger, for the pain that has come from her abuse.

"For centuries, our masculine culture has repressed her natural power, burnt her temples, and killed her priestesses. Through his drive for mastery, and his fear of the feminine—which he cannot understand or control—the patriarchy has not just neglected her, but deliberately tortured and destroyed. He has not just raped her, but torn the very fabric of life, the primal wholeness of which she is always the guardian.

"To welcome the feminine is to acknowledge and accept her pain and anger, and the part we have played in this desecration. Women have too often colluded with the masculine, denied their own power and natural magic, and instead accepted masculine values and ways of thinking. They have betrayed their own deepest self. But we must be careful not to become caught in this darkness, in the dynamics of abuse, the anger, and betrayal."

One of my dear friends, who is a man, wears a button that reads, "Men can stop rape." It's a concept that's not often discussed or explored. A complementary concept might be, "Women can reclaim their anger and power." We can and we will, using anger as a catalyst for transformation.

• Anger is a Tool of the Non-Aggressive Warrior

Synchronicity is a sacred confirmation that we are on the cusp of discovering an important truth. As I immersed myself in task of writing about anger, several events occurred. Anger reared its (not-so-) ugly head as an indicator of something that needs to be acknowledged and addressed during these times.

The first synchronicity was that several female clients focused on reclaiming and processing their anger in magnificent, transformative, and effective ways. My role was to remain strong and clear in my commitment to focus on the role of anger in reclaiming our power.

The second event was a group supervision in which anger showed up as the topic; most specifically, the role of suppressed anger in physical illness—psychosomatic and otherwise. What is clearly agreed on and supported by research is that anger must be acknowledged, claimed, and processed in the service of good mental health.

The third amazing occurrence was that a close friend strongly recommended Dr. Carolyn Baker's new book, *Navigating the Coming Chaos.* I ordered it immediately and when it arrived two days later, I was ready to devour the contents. I knew it contained the exact information I needed to complete this segment on anger.

Reviewing the table of contents, I encountered her captivating chapter titled "From Anger to Anguish—Anger as a Mindful Practice." This section included the necessary insights to solidify my hypothesis:

**Ignoring and denying our anger
greatly interferes with our process
of reclaiming our power as women.**

Accessing the energy of anger is required to do the work that must be done. Thank you, Carolyn, for your insights and the reminder. I unite with you as a solar sister acting on behalf of the planet.

Dr. Baker writes: "In some spiritual and psychological circles, we frequently hear unambiguous proscriptions against the emotion of anger. The taboo originates to some extent from a focus in those circles on ascendance, transcendence, and an aversion to descent. From that perspective people on a spiritual path are supposed to be kind and play nice all the time. The insistence on 'rising above' anger is no doubt another manifestation of disavowing soul and the body, preferring instead to distance oneself from the messy foibles of living in a body and having a complex repertoire of emotions."

She continues, "However, in many indigenous traditions, anger is not experienced with the same suspicion one finds in Western spiritual circles. While ancient teachings regarding anger do not condone aggression, they do not unequivocally assume that feeling the emotion of anger will lead to hostility or violence. In fact, they tend to revere anger as an innate human emotion, which may be utilized on behalf of the earth community without inflicting harm. Ancient teachings often include practices for 'uploading' the raw emotion of anger in higher chakras or physiological energy centers of behalf of preserving boundaries or protecting the innocent—both of which are characteristics of the non-aggressive warrior."

As you can see, there are many ways to view and use anger. It can be volatile, unpredictable, violent, explosive, relentless, cruel or used to control, manipulate, or dominate.

It is also one of the most effective methods of mobilizing and motivating. It is a catalyst—the means by which our mission as women is emblazoned on our souls, for our purpose is something we cannot afford to forget now that it has crystallized. As a propellant, anger is a necessary and essential skill set for our future. As women, it is crucial that we access our denied and self-directed anger now and learn how to use it effectively for positive, global change.

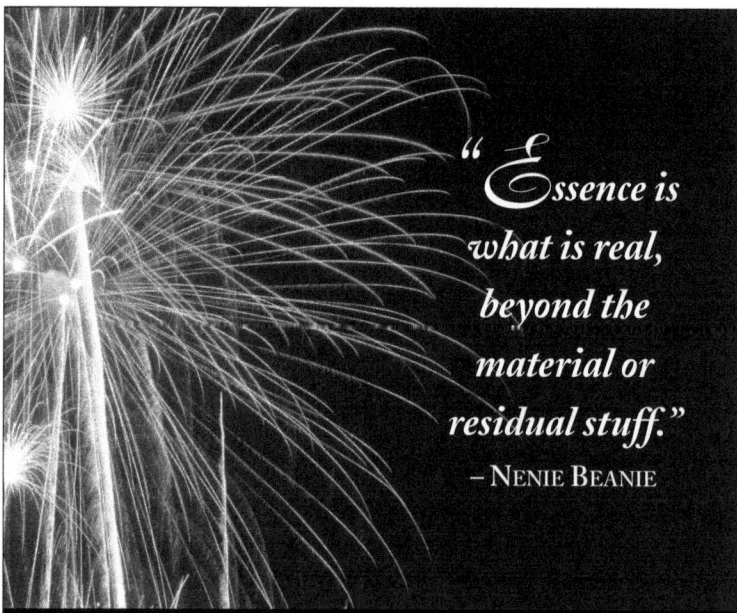

> "*Essence is what is real, beyond the material or residual stuff.*"
> – NENIE BEANIE

On Behalf of the Planet
Why Women? Why Now?

While sitting with a group of women, in a moment of absolutely clarity, one of them suddenly said, "We women are unplugging our energy from supporting the men to supporting each other." I gasped with the impart of the statement and exclaimed, "What a powerful energetic shift!"

As I continue to learn about how women of European descent had our roots severed during the "Burning Times," I see this dynamic as an important component to reclaim power.

As this holocaust forced us to relinquish our connection to Mother Earth, we shifted to a dependent relationship on men of European descent. Because the source of nourishment in our indigenous ways was violently taken from us, we became like parasites on the men who now held exclusive access to power, and to the Divine. We were relegated to servanthood, objectified, and had only men to rely on for survival and salvation.

We became disconnected from one another and moved our entire life force into the service of care-taking, adapting, and pleasing.

As the European males became progressively more affluent, and our usefulness became more ornamental, we began immersing ourselves in distractions such as shopping, decorating (ourselves and our environments), social events and mindless small talk.

Remaining dependent on men and distracting ourselves with materialism run amuck prevents us from doing the work that only we can do, which is reversing the destructive trajectory of our planet.

Why women? Why now? Because it is time.

> "*The solar feminine is true solar power.*"
> – NENIE BEANIE

Mother Earth Is Speaking Loudly

This piece was writting on a summer morning as I gathered with several women for the intention of listening to what Mother Earth wanted to tell us.

<u>PAT</u>: *It is my intent to create an energetic vortex and tune in to what you have to say.*

<u>MOTHER EARTH</u>: I am noisy like the wind. Crows are noisy. Thunder is noisy. Breathtaking bolts of lightning are accompanied by deafening cracks.

I hear you speaking in a loud, deafening, powerful voice. Are you saying that as women our voices must become loud and powerful to match the power you demonstrate during an extraordinary storm?

Of course, you know the urgency and the devastation in front of us. You know that women have been immersed in patriarchal cultures, and have deeply internalized disempowerment. You fear using the full power of your voices even though you understand the urgency.

I hear you saying, "Be loud. Be strong. Be relentless. Be unyielding." I hear you saying that this is the energy required of the feminine right now—the solar feminine that makes itself known in a loud and clear voice.

You are my daughters and I need you desperately now.

Women Acting on Behalf of the Planet

Remember the expression, "My blood is boiling?" What a powerful phrase.

My blood was boiling the day my credit card company restricted my card because they hadn't received a $2 payment. No amount of reasoning with the customer service department yielded a response other than, "These are the rules." Blood boiling.

In the summer of 2010, British Petroleum (BP) blasted millions and millions of gallons of oil into the Gulf of Mexico. Mother Earth's blood was boiling. Indescribable and immeasurable death and destruction was caused by their actions, taken in the service of monetary gain. Just as credit card companies charge obscene interest rates of 18-30%, there appears to be no end to the degree to which the patriarch will go for profit.

In these circumstances, is it really more "spiritual" to deny our anger? Is anger something to transcend and avoid at all costs?

Credit card interest rates don't enrage you? Okay. Oils spills don't trigger a spark of fury? Okay. How about a heinous war technique used in Bosnia and the Congo targeted at women? One that includes sewing dead animals in their vaginas? Do you feel the anger now?

Let me ask: is it possible that denying our anger to ourselves and others keeps us passive and ineffective?

We have such powerful role models in nature of female ferocity. Mother Bear fierceness is practically a cliché. Everyone knows that any mother protecting her cubs is a force with which to be reckoned. In her presentations, Marianne Williamson frequently shares that mother hyenas will encircle the babies, effectively protecting them from the males attempting to take their food. She then proclaims in a powerful voice, "Surely, the women of America can do better than hyenas."

How absurd it is that our planet is being destroyed by greed, millions of children are starving to death daily, and millions of women are raped and murdered and we're not angry? Think about it: how crazy is that?

In her classic *Trauma and Recovery,* Judith Herman states that we live in denial about trauma because so many atrocities are just too difficult to maintain in our consciousness. We can't walk around enraged and agitated all the time. Our systems would burn out.

So what do we do? We find whatever ways we can to access as much strong, healthy, clear power as we possibly can. We stand in our own power, and we collaborate with other women.

Margaret Paul, author of *Inner Bonding,* articulates the difference between anger and what she calls outrage from essence, "which is the response of a true loving adult to injustice."

We form an enormous nation of women standing up, standing strong, standing powerfully in action in the service of the planet and all her inhabitants. In doing so, we show the world that, yes, we women CAN do better than hyenas.

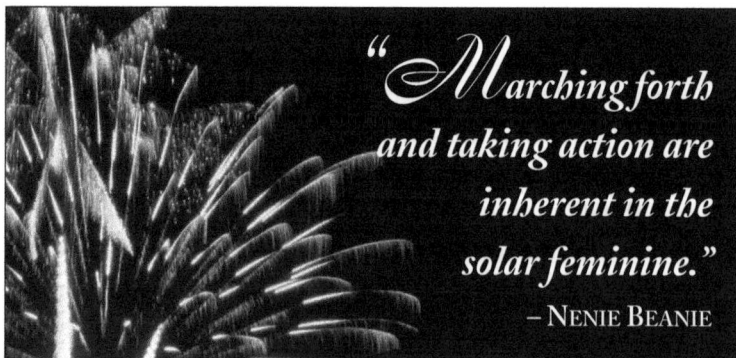

> "*Marching forth and taking action are inherent in the solar feminine.*"
> – NENIE BEANIE

It's Push Time

How we engage the urgency of these times is the most important decision each of us can make. Jean Houston says, "These are the most important times in human history. This is the time when we decide whether we live or whether we die."

This is truly the 11th hour. There is no time for sloppiness, laziness, or procrastination. This is not the year to make another resolution for another diet or another exercise program. This is the time to ask yourself:

- Who am I?
- What do I love?
- What am I here to offer the planet?
- What are my Sacred Marching Orders?

It's time to go deeply within yourself, connect with your soul, and ask. "What did I come to the planet to give and how do I offer it now?" You didn't show up at this time on the planet by accident. You're here because you have a unique contribution to make. First nation people taught about the concept of "original medicine."

Original medicine is the unique alchemy of the gifts and talents you were born with combined with the skills and experiences gained during your lifetime. The teaching concludes that each person's original medicine is unique and if they don't offer it to the world, it is lost forever.

The Hopi Elders wrote, "We are the ones we've been waiting for." As we are catapulted toward 2012, we need to know in the deepest levels of our souls that it is "push time." Vikki Hanchin of WholePersonWholePlanet.com describes "push time" in this way: "When everything in your being rallies in the act of creation."

We're midwifing a New Earth. It's time to stand fully in

your power, offering your original medicine in the service of the planet. It's "PUSH TIME."

Connection To Ourselves Via Connection to Mother Earth
by Robin Milam

Robin's story offers a powerful example of a woman following her sacred marching orders. She walks ahead and shows us the way.

My trips to the rainforest and my deep connection with forests, rocks, and rivers show me so clearly that our planet needs us as never before. Our planet calls us to re-examine our relationship with the natural world around us. We are not just on this Earth; we are of this Earth and are deeply connected to every element.

Our planet is crying to be nurtured, to be honored. It is time for us to recognize that nature also has rights to be protected in much the same way as we protect the rights of humans and even corporations.

Those of us in the modern world have lost our connection to Earth on so many levels. Yet what we see and think and speak—our choices of lifestyle, food, transportation, and so much more—affects everything around us. This speaks to the condition of the earth today, and also to the yearning many of us feel to go beyond our material focus toward a deeper spiritual connection.

When we reconnect to our inner guide—our own Self, our Soul, when we can have the core essence connection— we connect with Earth and all life, as well.

I am a voice for our planet, for humanity, and for each of us reconnecting deeply with our own inner voice. When we're in that space, we honor the diversity of our global cultures and our own uniqueness. We recognize that we are all connected to Mother Earth, that we are actually of the earth. From that space we nurture a world that works for all, a world of love, of respect and honor, of nourishment, and beauty.

I recently read a beautiful book by Bill McKibben called *Eaarth* – Earth spelled E-a-a-r-t-h. McKibben makes the point that Earth as we knew it ten years ago, no longer exists. The hope is that by stepping back and opening ourselves, we may be able to break the automatic and destructive course we are on. Why do we have to have bigger and better? The greatest value of life is in those simple things nearest and dearest to us.

In April 2010, I attended the first *People's Conference on Climate Change and the Rights of Mother Earth* in Cochabamba, Bolivia. My intention for the trip was to capture stories of women at the conference. I videotaped a small number of women answering my questions: What brings you to Cochabamba now? What gives you hope? Some were young women in their 20s, some were grandmothers in their 60s and 70s.

Their responses were very moving and consistent. One woman said, "It is time for women to speak up, to have our voices heard in a way that has not happened for many centuries. The time is now because we women are the mother energy, the nurturing creative energy, and this is what our planet and humanity needs."

When I asked the women "What gives you hope?" a few welled up with tears. They are emboldened by a new listening for the feminine voice. One woman said, "What gives me hope is you asking me these questions and the fact that we are being heard." These women are fully awake and alive to the difference they make by speaking their truth. These are women who continually reclaim their power through listening deeply and speaking the wisdom of their heart.

We are starting to see shifts toward valuing the feminine perspective in a profound way. Globally we recognize that honoring and listening to the feminine—in balance with the masculine—really does create a more sustainable, thriving world that works for all.

When we give too much priority to either the masculine or the feminine, when we swing the pendulum too far in either direction, we create an out-of-balance scenario. Because masculine has dominated for so long, many people are living in a space of overwhelm, anxiety, and despair.

Let's be clear, this is not about men versus women. This is about allowing the feminine elements of intuition, holistic thinking, receptivity, feeling deeply and nurturing to regain their rightful balance with the analytical masculine intellect—the wisdom of the heart to be in balance with wisdom of the mind.

My trips to the Amazon are life-altering experiences because the rainforest is such a feminine place. She is the womb of our planet. The rainforest has a fiercely gentle way of heart opening and bringing us home to ourselves. The deep wisdom that the Achuar and other indigenous peoples display is rooted in their innate connection with the natural world.

When I get out of the little airplane on a dirt runway, walk down the embankment to the river, and canoe the last leg of the journey to Kapawi Lodge, something happens to me. As a matter of fact, even now when I'm describing it, I can feel this sweet powerful energy rising in me that is my connection with the feminine in balance. In that space, I feel deeply nurtured and at home with myself.

When I leave the rainforest, fly home and greet the sprawling electricity of the city around me, it's jolting. In that jolt, I recognize that in our identity with everything materialistic—and this pace of go, go, go to make money to live comfortably—lies a deep cellular disconnect. In that disconnect arises a hunger—the hunger emerging now—to open and awaken our spirituality, and especially our awareness of the value of feminine balance in our lives. When we reconnect to our feminine essence, we connect to the space where we nurture and honor and renew ourselves.

Women as a Force of Nature

Throughout the writing process of this book, I remained committed to conveying a sense of urgency without eliciting fear. As you read further, I invite you to hear this message with the vehement urgency with which it is written. Let me highlight the most crucial elements of these extraordinary times.

"It's all about energy," Carolyn Myss writes. She continues, "If you're not thinking in terms of energy, you're missing 99% of it."

Great information, but what do we do with it?

As energetic beings living in a universe of energy, there are numerous methods to recharging. One of the most concrete, valuable, and tangible ways to refuel is to focus on beauty. And the beauty of nature is definitely the most powerful source of renewal. Plugging ourselves into the beauty and energy field of the natural world nourishes us and raises our vibration—simple, clear, concrete, something we can consciously choose. This exercise reestablishes our deep powerful knowing of the sacredness of all life, restoring our severed roots, for ourselves and for all life.

In *Waking the Global Heart,* Anodea Judith writes, "To pull the roots of survival out of their earthen bed and wrap them instead around the clouds of heaven took a force equal in power to birth. What cosmic power could possibly break the archaic spell of the Mother and the seamless unity with nature? Only the fear generated by death was potent enough to rally consciousness in a whole new direction. Not that this choice was made consciously, for who in their right minds would choose death over life, violence over peace, and fear over security? Yet, for reasons we would do well to understand, history has made it abundantly clear that humans have made such choices repeatedly. We still do today."

During a recent retreat, we went to the woods to connect with a chosen tree. Leah came back with an image on her phone and said, "This is an example of the urgency that must drive our actions." She then showed a picture of a dead raccoon with an arrow through her neck. This animal had obviously been killed for sport and left to rot on the side of the road. This is an energy that does not acknowledge the sacredness of life. This is an energy that has placed all life on a high-speed trajectory toward death and destruction.

In *The Return of the Feminine and the World Soul,* Llewellyn Vaughn-Lee writes, "The innate wisdom of the feminine is needed to repair the damage we have done and reconnect with what is sacred and essential within ourselves and within life. We need to understand our part within the sacred web of life, and how to relate once again, to this primal wholeness that is a direct expression of the oneness of the divine."

He warns us, "It may be painful to be fully present, to hold the sacred connection with life, the earth, and our own soul. But, without the presence of the sacred feminine and those who honor it within themselves, an essential substance will be lost to life. The spark of the divine that connects the creation to the Creator—the spark that holds the mystery of creation and the divine purpose of everything; every butterfly, every stone, the laughter of every child, and every lover's tear—will begin to dim."

As I write, my dog Daisy is lying in front of the fireplace, breathing peacefully, maybe dreaming of running in the woods. During the female holocaust, women could be tortured and killed for loving animals or walking alone in the woods. Some say women are a bridge between heaven and earth. It occurs to me that animals may be a bridge between us and the energy of Gaia, Mother Earth. Because the function of the burning times was to sever the roots of the feminine in nature worshipping, goddess worshipping cultures. It seems obvious that eliminating the connection between animals and women would be a crucial component to that end.

It's almost a stereotype that a single woman over 50-years-old has a dog. Some may theorize that having a creature to nurture is the reason; that may be part of it. More importantly, having a dog gets us out in the woods, by the rivers, and connecting with each other.

I have a neighbor with whom I frequently walk who has become like a sponge for our conversations about the divine feminine. Our dogs connect us and our power grows. Animals are bridges in these two important ways: connecting us with nature, and connecting us with each other. Even dogs are playing their part in fueling the role of the collective feminine in planetary awakening!

A few years ago I went into the woods with the intention of choosing a tree to listen to. As I sat with my root chakra at the base of the tree, these words came clearly: She said, "Look up and around you and see how all the branches are interconnected with one another. The same is true of the roots below the earth that you cannot see. Connect with these roots. Way too much attention has been given to Father Sky; it is now time to pay attention to Mother Earth."

In Jean Shinoda Bolen's introduction to her book *Like a Tree*, she writes, "The exercise of dominion over women and girls can take many forms: trafficking, female genital mutilation, stoning, honor killings, or selling daughters to settle a debt. Closer to home, women and girls are dominated and demeaned through domestic violence, rape, and the sexual abuse of children. Physically and psychologically, when a girl or woman is treated as property, she is 'like a tree'—or the dog or horse that can be valued, loved, and treated well, or worked, beaten, and sold. These are patterns and behaviors rooted in raising boys to identify with the aggressor and raising girls to learn powerlessness. These are distortions of natural growth."

As we women reclaim our sacred connection with Mother Earth and all life, we reclaim our power and with the force of Mother Nature say, "Enough is enough!"

As we do this, we reverse the trajectory of death and destruction that dims the force field on the planet. As Llewellyn Vaughn-Lee writes, "As matter becomes realigned to it's divine nature, it vibrates at a higher frequency. It begins to sing and this song is one of the ways it will heal itself."

It is up to us women now—who carry the memories of the forces that quieted us—to reclaim our power with a fierceness that demonstrates the capacity to reverse this trajectory of death prevailing over the sacredness of life. Only we can do this, because we women are a force of nature as we restore our roots and reclaim the sacredness of the natural world.

❧❖❧

"As I sit with the BP disaster, other emotions course through my body—deep grief, despair, and helplessness. I have to wonder about the emotions of the earth itself. And since I believe that Gaia is a living, breathing organism, I must correct my use of 'the earth itself' and state unequivocally that She must be very, very angry. While we cannot validate with certainty the earth's anger, we can certainly attest to our own in the face of humanity's devastation of the ecosystems."
– DR. CAROLYN BAKER

❧❖❧

Plugging Into the Energy of Awe

As I sit in the energy of this moment, I look out my window and catch my breath at the image of the sun bursting through the billowy white and grey clouds with the tree tops framing the picture.

I actually feel my energy expanding and I recognize that I have plugged into the energy of awe. My breathing deepens and expands, my eyes widen, and my cells celebrate. This connection with the natural world expands exponentially.

I can't turn away from this image—this perfect picture

of nature. I feel mesmerized, gazing, heart wide open like a lover who is captivated by the sight of her beloved. The boundaries of my individual self dissolve and I feel the energetic lines emanating out from my Core Essence Self, beyond space and time into a merging with the scene I behold. I am now a part of it, and it a part of me.

This is the experience of plugging into the energy of awe. Knowing—feeling the Oneness of the Allness is accelerated by this practice of plugging into the energy of awe. It's as if my cells and my energy lines merge with the energy of the beautiful aspects of nature I observe.

I feel like a mother gazing at her newborn and the newborn gazing at her mother, simultaneously. I experientially know what sacred teachings proclaim, "It is all One and the Divine lives in everything, and there is no division between the Divine and me." I continue to advance and expand in my understanding and experiencing the Oneness.

As I learn and experience the fullness of this, I feel prompted to offer one of the gifts I carry—that of making the abstract concrete. With this intention I offer to you, dear reader, this concrete information.

Catching oneself in moments of awe and consciously plugging into that energy field assists you in your desire to return home to the Oneness.

Whenever you can, plug into the Energy of Awe. It serves you. It serves the planet. It helps bring us all Home.

Apology Letter to Mother Earth

On the morning of one Valentine's Day, I was prompted to write a love letter to Mother Earth.

The degree to which we take this beautiful planet for

granted and the level to which we exploit her cannot be put into words. How do you write a love letter to someone you've defiled, exploited, violated and ignored? The obvious answer is that an apology must come first. So instead of a love letter I am writing an apology letter.

～◦❀◦～

Dear Mother Earth ~

I feel my heart ache as I write this. The pain begins as I actively move myself out of the denial of ignoring the amount of desecration that has already occurred and continues on a daily basis. The pain of acknowledgement is almost too much to bear.

I reflect on a statement made by a friend recently. She said, "If you are quiet enough, you can hear Mother Earth scream." The truth is, we are usually never quiet enough.

The movie **Avatar** *opens with the words, "They killed their mother." We as a human species are headed down a path of matricide. I suspect we must feel the pain of what we are doing before we can wake up to this unspeakable reality.*

As I continued watching **Avatar**, *mesmerized by the beauty and connection with the natural world they lived in, I became progressively more emotionally engaged with the screen. These images became so real for me that when their Mother Tree was annihilated, I felt like my heart was being ripped through my chest.*

The intersection between the movie screen and real life became so real that I could hardly breathe.

Unfortunately, I did what everyone else did when it was over. I walked out of the movie and back into my everyday life.

I go on about my business and you continue to be raped, pillaged, and ultimately destroyed. Ignoring and denying allows us all to function and also allows unprecedented abuses of you continue on and on until ultimate annihilation of us all.

Now what? Happy talk and new age jargon doesn't fit here. Marianne Williamson frequently quoted the Course in Miracles *by saying that we must look at the crucifixion but not remain there. How do we move from the crucifixion (this time, of you, our Mother) to the resurrection (the birth of a New Earth)?*

Fervently in your service,

Patricia Fero

As I continued to write, I noticed that my apology letter moved away from addressing Mother Earth and into an exploration of what we do next.

We're now moving from the problem to the solution.

Andrew Harvey, who initiated *Sacred Activism,* suggested we find what causes our hearts to break and move our passion into that cause. Can any of us look around at the plight of the planet and the sentient beings we share it with and not feel the heart break?

This is the 11th hour. Time is running out for us and the consequences of not taking action are dire.

How do we activate this energy field? We listen within for our individual "marching orders" and we march forth collectively in the service of our beloved Mother. The troops are activated. Women of the world arise. We have a planet to save. Now is the time and we are the Women!

Solar Feminine Rising

The Dalai Lama issued a proclamation at the Vancouver Peace Summit in the Fall of 2009 saying, "The world will be saved by the western woman." Now Archbishop Tutu has joined forces with him in agreement with this statement. Why do these powerful men make this announcement, and how is this related to the solar feminine?

The solar feminine is about activating the lower three chakras, as well as the fifth, or throat chakra. Thousands of years of subjugation of women prevented access to these chakras.

There is no arguing about the power and benefit of the heart chakra. The power of love, activated through the heart chakra is undeniably the most powerful force in the universe. However, the loss of access to these other four chakras has crippled us. Activating the solar feminine is reclaiming these four chakras (the first three mentioned in Chapter 2):

1. The root, first chakra, represented by the color red, is associated with groundedness in the earth.

2. The sacral, second chakra, represented by the color orange, is associated with sexuality, creativity and passion.

3. The solar plexus, third chakra, represented by the color yellow, is associated with power and will.

4. The throat, fifth chakra, represented by the color blue, is associated with the voice.

Many women have a pattern of loving men who do not treat us well. We seek love and harmony at any cost to ourselves. These behaviors are related to lack of access to these four chakras and being relegated exclusively to the heart chakra by the dominant culture.

This arrangement has served the patriarchy well. They experience no accountability, their children are well cared for, and their houses are made beautiful and comfortable—all in the service of maintaining the status quo. The heart can serve the patriarchy very well—at great cost to ourselves and the loss of most of our capabilities and autonomy.

What happened when we became less dependent on men as a result of birth control and access to the workplace? Could this have been an integral part of things beginning to change?

Access to birth control allows a woman to have more personal choice. She begins to control her own destiny. Access to the workplace releases another layer of dependence on men for physical survival. These two factors may be the most important sociological factors in moving us toward realization of the statement made by the Dalai Lama.

We see stirrings of the re-activation of the throat chakra and the third chakra of power and will. The second chakra, which holds the energy of sexuality, creativity, and passion burst forth naturally as birth control became available and womens' sexuality was returned to the rightful owners: each individual woman.

The cultural phenomenon of rape under patriarchal reign remains the most effective way to decimate the power of women. Throughout the past 5,000 years, womens' power has been most effectively taken from them through this method, especially prior to adulthood. Incidents of childhood sexual abuse and date rape in college are astronomical.

Last, but certainly not least, is the root chakra. This is the powerful red chakra that grounds us with the earth.

The earth has been called Mother for as long as we can ascertain: being a woman, the creatrix of life, being grounded deeply into the Great Mother, the true origin of all life. What could be more powerful? As we reestablish our connection, access and realize our true power as women with Mother earth and the Divine Mother, we come to know ourselves as women truly standing in our power.

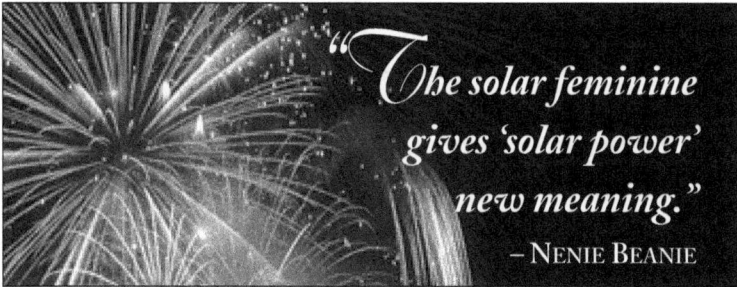

"The solar feminine gives 'solar power' new meaning."

– NENIE BEANIE

Joining Forces As Alpha Females

One of the most powerful stories of sisters loving sisters is the story of my dear friend, Marie. Three weeks after her beautiful 18-year-old daughter began school as a freshman at Michigan State University, her daughter Jackie died suddenly while preparing to go out with three girlfriends on a Saturday night. There were no drugs involved, but her heart stopped beating (a valve closed), and she was gone before she hit the floor.

Jackie was Marie's only daughter and she raised her magnificently as a single mother. Jackie was the center of Marie's life and nurturing her into adulthood was Marie's deepest commitment.

When Jackie died, Marie called on the support of her women friends. Being a woman who always had crystal-clarity about what she needed, Marie let us know that our first act of support would be to go with her to the funeral home to claim Jackie's ashes. So, three days after her daughter died, Marie sat in the front seat of a big van carrying seven other women, heading to pick up the remains of her daughter.

Orchestrated as always by Marie, she directed us to wait in the family waiting room while she received the ashes. When she was ready, we would join her. Two friends walked into the main room while the rest of us waited. Waiting is an inadequate word because each of us, with every fiber or our being, was holding up Marie with our love. We waited. Abruptly, one of her friends who had gone in with her, ran out saying, "She needs you."

We rushed into the room and surrounded Marie, who sat crumbled at the table that held the wooden box containing the ashes. She embraced the box and we engulfed her with our love. All nine of us were loving and holding Marie. All of us, simultaneously sending her the most powerful love we could muster. Marie picked up the box of Jackie and headed for the van. We followed, and loved and prayed for the strength to play our role in helping Marie survive this moment.

We drove in silence to one of the women's houses and settled ourselves around a giant dining room table where we began to feast together as is so often done after funerals. Marie sat at the head of the table and we all began telling Jackie stories. Most of these women had been with Marie since her pregnancy and been a powerful net of support for her in her journey as a single mom.

In the midst of this energy, I commented to Marie that her friends were all so different, but each loved her so much. She was quick and clear in her response, "My friends are very different, but they all have one thing in common. They are strong women." This planted a seed in me that sprouted the next day and bloomed at Jackie's memorial the following day.

When it was my turn to speak, I walked to the podium, connected with my Core Essence Self, and spoke from the bottom of my soul. I looked directly at Marie and said, "Last night at our gathering I was struck by the awareness that you are an Alpha female who surrounds herself with Alpha females. From all the power that contains, I want you to know that 'We gotcha! We gotcha.'" I held my arms in a gesture of embrace. At that moment, this collective of Alpha females was committed to supporting and holding up Marie.

The awareness of Alpha females supporting Alpha females carries the same significance as the realization that women are moving energy from supporting men to supporting other women, which I described earlier.

This energy is required to do what needs to be done for the planet and her inhabitants. Sisters loving sisters is not simply a pleasant concept, but an enormously powerful energy field that is the catalyst for creating a New Earth.

Lunar and Solar Collaborating on Behalf of the Planet

In 1991, studies at the University of Connecticut found that the stress response in women was not the well-known flight or fight response we were all taught in school. Researchers there discovered that the female response to stress is tend and befriend. They learned that this "tend and befriend" reaction is fueled by oxytocin, the bonding hormone.

Tend and befriend is wonderful, powerful, and beautifully effective, but I submit that this oxytocin response must be turned all the way up to Mother Bear

Fierceness, at least intermittently, because the urgency required really is that of turning around the Titanic before it hits the iceberg.

Tend and befriend is the energy with which we will do this, but with the single pointed laser-focus and energy of Mother Bear Fierceness.

The condition of the planet—brought on by our choices—requires the highest commitment to reversing our current course and moving ourselves into the unity and oneness that has been predicted by all the great religions and spiritual teachers.

Celebrating Our Strengths

If we're not competing with our sisters, fitting into the template that patriarchy has created for us, we're free to love our sisters. The power of women collaborating—sisters loving each other with support—is the primary key to planetary transformation. When we do it through powerful love in action, everyone benefits.

Under patriarchy for the past 5,000 years, women have been socialized to serve men and quiet our voices in the service of their goals. To energetically unplug from that system and to move instead into a system of collaboration with our sisters is exactly what our planet requires to reverse the destructive trajectory of patriarchy.

When I express my views on this pattern, I am often met with resistance from both women and men. My response is that if a house is on fire, the critical question is not, "Who set the fire?" but "Where is the water to douse it?" At this unprecedented time, women in collaboration have the resources to create the necessary shift, aka put out the fire.

Loving our sisters is about seeing the beauty and power

in other women and living from the energy of supporting them as they come to discover their own power and beauty. We have been socialized to diminish ourselves and feel invisible. As we love our sisters, we see each other into visibility and into the reclamation of our lost power. This power is necessary to be reclaimed, embodied, and used in the service of worldwide transformation.

We love our sisters by seeing them as sisters and not as competitors. We love our sisters by mirroring for them their magnificence. We love our sisters by supporting them in the actions taken on their own behalf. We love our sisters by standing in our own power, offering them a reflection of theirs. We love our sisters and all life by working in collaboration with them toward the greater good of the planet.

Stepping out of competition and into collaboration is the essence of what the world needs now.

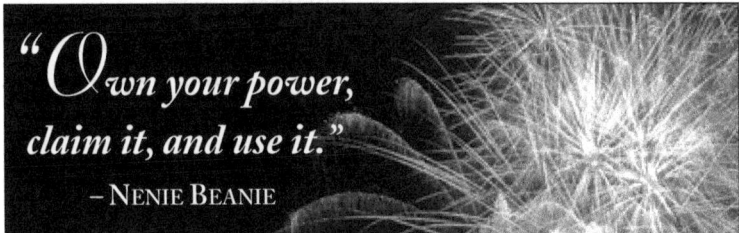

> "*Own your power, claim it, and use it.*"
> – NENIE BEANIE

Seeing Each Other Into Visibility

While I dated an African-American man, I noticed that whenever we passed another African-American male, they would exchange greetings. There was a nod of the head, a verbal acknowledgement, and a clear direct eye-to-eye contact. I found myself very attracted to this custom, although I didn't fully understand why at the time. Since then, I've come to understand more.

When someone is a member of an oppressed group in a dominant culture, they become largely invisible to the dominant society. My friend—and those he greeted—understood this wound of invisibility and offered each other the gift of being seen as well as the gift of connection. The power of being seen by another—especially as it counteracts the wound of invisibility—is monumental.

This is what I believe women—as an invisible group in our dominator culture—can do for each other.

However, there is a twist to women's invisibility. The dominant culture not only asks women to be sexual, supportive, and serving, but to also silence our authentic self. The social veneer, which includes beauty, efficiency, long-suffering, and care-taking, is very much encouraged. This false self is invited, even paraded, certainly not invisible, then exploited and controlled. So the invisibility required is of the authentic self.

What a deplorable fate: to expend our precious life force to meet the social expectation of women. It starves us psychically and is part of the pattern of exploitation that threatens the earth itself. Competing with one another to rank higher in social facade is surely the wrong direction.

The call to authenticity is very strong in women now. Many women are participating in circles where authentic expression is invited and received as the sacredness of life itself. We are seeing each other into visibility, making direct eye contact with who we really are.

The Solar Enters
by Beth Blevins

In the spring of 2007, I received a series of visions of
women creating peace. The following occurred during a
group meditation.

At night, in a trim suburban neighborhood, in each front
yard along a street, a woman stands alone. Each woman
stiffly faces the street, her house behind her. On both sides
of the street, for blocks, woman after woman after woman,
one stands in each yard. The women could see each other if
they looked, but they don't; they stand silently, staring
straight ahead or with heads bent, lost in a great,
devastating grief.

Suddenly, lively columns of light—bright, colorful,
igniting, shimmering, a cross between fireworks and the
northern lights—begin to descend from the night sky. One
by one, each column finds its way to one of the women and
slips over her. The women look up and around with wonder
at these fantastic columns, extending their hands to touch
it, watching the light dance off their skin.

Slow smiles come to their faces as each woman discovers her neighbor, encased in her own enchanting column of light. Their eyes meet and their smiles widen. Each woman in her column begins to joyfully twirl and spin. Once all of the women are spinning, the columns gravitate toward each other and merge into one great column, one great gathering. The beauty of the light is astounding, the brilliance of the smiles astonishing! The women are no longer alone and in pain but merged as collective joy.

There will be a global cleansing of tears, I was told. As each woman hears the message of her part in the global transformation and understands the implications of leaving the old ways behind—what can appear as "sacrifice"—she will cry. Masses of women will begin crying when they face this understanding. And these tears, this mass crying, will cleanse the Mother Earth and perform a restorative, healing function. This in turn, will bring back the remembrance of a joy that has long been forgotten, a joy stored so deeply in the heart that it was as lost—the sacred joy of the Great Mother.

> *"Love is the most powerful force in the universe."*
> – NENIE BEANIE

Collaboration
By Beth Blevins

In a group meditation, I asked how I may serve the Sacred
Feminine and the following was shown to me.

I saw two women on a tandem bicycle. They wore
simple white robes belted at the waist—the daily, working
garb of a priestess or guardian. The women pedaled along
until they arrived at their destination, which was a vortex
of two great spiraling, intertwining columns of white light
ascending into the heavens. They got off their bicycle and
parked it neatly. Then, with a certain and purposeful stride,
they walked directly into the center of the vortex. Each
stood still and expectant, surrounded by the spiraling
beams of light, and simply allowed herself to float up

within the column into the night heavens. There they hovered, watching over the Earth.

The scene was suddenly interrupted, and I saw myself going through a fast-food drive-thru. When I ordered, pictures in cartoon dialog bubbles appeared rather than spoken words. First, a bubble with one soft drink appeared, then a bubble with a hamburger, and lastly, a bubble with a book! Although it seemed a strange combination, I comprehended the meaning of the pictures immediately. I understood that I would never again order only one of each item. From this point on, I, or we (you and I), will always order two or more because we will be "feeding" more than ourselves. In other words, what we do, we do for the world. We are to work in pairs and groups now. Being concerned with individual needs and concerns is the old way; the cosmic shift that is bringing about the return of the Sacred Feminine is propelling us into the collective heart and mind. We are ushering in the age of the collective—a collaborative model of peace, harmony, and balance. It is time for this that is written in the cosmic records to manifest.

Then I suddenly returned to the scene of the two women, seeing them still hovering in the heavens above the Earth. I heard the word "over-soul" and began to receive instructions from them. The first was that we are now to work with the "over-souls." (I had heard of this word, but wasn't sure of its exact meaning at the time—see note on page 92.) From now on, we will be much more aware of the separation between our soul and our body; we will be working directly on the soul level rather than at the physical or even psychic level. Communication will be coming in directly through our crown chakras, not as much through our third eye or solar plexus or any other of our "filters" (eyes, ears, mind, etc.) anymore. It is time for us to give up these filters into the cosmos. To do this, we can meditate, lying flat on our backs with our legs spread slightly apart and our arms at 30 to 40 degree angles from our bodies. During the meditation, we must willingly release these filters, or senses, to the One. We will feel a drawing out and tingling sensation when this happens. (I was instructed to lay down after the meditation and experience it.)

They confirmed my understanding that group meditations are becoming more powerful and individual meditations less. I was told that it is important to meditate as a collective; however, it is no longer always necessary to be together physically or even connected by telephone. We can agree on a specific time to meditate and at that time, as we sit individually, we can speak each woman's name aloud, which will create a connection with each other. We have reached the point where we have the ability to do this and will feel a palpable connection with the others when we do so.

Then I saw the two women riding their tandem bike down a road and others joining them as they traveled along. The instructions came that we are to "go on the road" spreading the message of the great transformation time of the Mother Earth, the re-emergence of the Sacred Feminine. Our work has accelerated the transformative energies faster than anticipated. Because of our commitment, love, and power, we have created a portal of opportunity to bring an even greater than expected smoothing or gentling of the global shift, the rebirthing. However, we must jump now at this opportunity and commit even more deeply. Our time of preparation as vessels of peace has finished sooner than expected. Practice is over; the work begins!

Note from Wikipedia: "...The term "Over-soul" is understood as the collective indivisible Soul, of which all individual souls or identities are included. The experience of this underlying reality of the indivisible "I am" state of the Over-soul is said to be veiled from the human mind by sanskaras, or impressions, acquired over the course of evolution and reincarnation. Thus the world, as it is perceived through the impressions of the past appears plural, while reality experienced in the present, unencumbered by past impressions (the unconditioned or liberated mind), perceives itself as the One indivisible totality."

5

High Noon

It's High Noon. By now you understand what the solar feminine is, and the value and necessity of activating the solar feminine within.

This chapter includes practical tips for activating your own solar feminine.

The more you practice this skill, the more you create an energetic gridwork for other women to map to. As we do this important work, we exponentially expand the energy of the solar feminine and draw in multi-dimensional support to assist us in serving the planet.

The Emergence of the Solar Feminine

A friend once shared a story with me about her spiritual teacher who had just completed a book when a new understanding came to him. He discarded the entire manuscript and started over. Writing a book at this time of monumental transition on the planet is no small feat. Every aspect of life is changing so rapidly, it's mind-boggling. Like never before, it is near-impossible to capture the essence of anything now that is lasting because we are in a state of dramatic flux.

My first rendition of this book, which was entitled *Sisters Stewarding the Shift,* was like meandering down a lazy river. In dramatic contrast, this new book is more akin to white water rafting.

The work that needs to be done on the planet requires a ferocity of energy, and a quality of commitment that only military language describes. The energy and effort a woman uses in the last few contractions as she pushes out her baby is a comparable metaphor. Whether it is experienced through the lens of the solar or the lunar, IT'S SHOWTIME! The troops are activated, on the field, and all the energies available to us, in whatever form, are being called on now.

We must show up, show up in legions, and show up now! We're past the 11th hour. It's showtime. It's on. If you're alive and you don't feel the urgency, step aside. There is a job to be done and the time to do it is now. We—and future generations—depend on our powerful action at this pivotal time in our evolution.

Power Tools for Accessing the Solar Feminine

Because the solar feminine is accessed through the activation of the lower three chakras, as well as the throat chakra, having specific power tools can be helpful. Let's take a closer look at these chakras individually and what you can do to ignite them within yourself.

• Root (First) Chakra

The root chakra is the energy center that is identified with grounding into the earth. Here are several ways to activate the root chakra:

1. Spend time in natural settings, particularly in forests. Connect with the energy of the roots and the trunks of the trees.

2. Stand with your back against the trunk of a chosen tree and feel your energetic roots going deep into the earth.

3. Sit on a rock, preferably, a boulder, and feel the connection of your root chakra with the rock. Feel yourself as the rock.

• *Sacral (Second) Chakra*

The sacral chakra is the energy center that houses your sexuality and creativity. Here are several ways to activate the sacral chakra:

1. Honor your sexual feelings and own them as your own.

2. Express yourself creatively. Explore what makes you feel enlivened. Allow yourself time to fully engage in these activities.

• *Solar Plexus (Third) Chakra*

The solar plexus chakra is related to power, will, and self awareness. Carolyn Myss says that this is the most important chakra of them all because this is where our personal power and sense of self resides. This is an area that has been lost to us under patriarchy. Here are several ways to activate the sacral chakra:

1. Say, "No," when you want to, and pay attention to how you feel physically when you do this.

2. Pay attention to—and allow—all your feelings. They are most often activated and present in the solar plexus area.

3. Pay attention to your intuition. Trust your gut feelings. Give them credibility by taking immediate and inspired action when appropriate.

• *Throat (Fifth) Chakra*

The throat chakra is the energy center connected to the voice. The loss of our voices as women is monumental. Regaining our voices is a monumental leap forward in our evolution as women and for the benefit of the world. Here are several ways to activate the throat chakra:

1. Become a regular member of a women's circle that practices circle principles. It is here that we hear ourselves into our voices.

2. Focus on role models of powerful women speaking truth.

3. Practice speaking your truth and notice how you feel when you do it. Then honor your feelings.

The activation of these chakras is crucial to the solar feminine awakening. These techniques are not difficult, but they do require an inward laser-focus as a constant assessment tool. The most prominent and easy question you can ask yourself in any moment is: "How am I feeling?" and tune in to the wisdom that is ready to inspire your next appropriate action.

> *"All the teachings speak about being still, slowing down, going deep."*
> – NENIE BEANIE

Language of the Lunar and Solar

Paying attention to the words we hear ourselves think or speak, and raising our awareness of the different languages of the lunar and solar, are effective ways to further ignite our solar feminine.

Dr. Masaru Emoto, famed water researcher, water crystal photographer, and author of *The Hidden Messages in Water* says, "The vibrational aspects of a word impart physical effects." Words carry energy. A heightened awareness of not only the words, but the energy behind the words, fuels the activation of the solar feminine within.

As you become more aware of your solar awakening, your language will change. You will be more direct and specific. You will use fewer words to convey your meanings with more efficiency. Your language will be action-oriented; clear communication will become a priority. Notice the subtle and not-so-subtle changes within yourself and others. It's no accident that every aspect of you is shifting in response to the solar feminine.

GO with it.
EMBRACE it.
BREATHE into it.

Following are just a few examples of these two distinct languages:

LUNAR LANGUAGE	SOLAR LANGUAGE
Receptive	Powerful
Nurturing	Direct
Inclusive	Active
Embracing	Action-oriented
Allowing	Initiative
Yielding	Bold
Surrendering	Standing firm
Inviting	Holding ground
Enfolding	Marching forward
Expansive	Strategizing
	Laser-focused

Illuminations of the Solar Feminine

Throughout the book-writing process, it became clear to me that this book would be a catalyst for the energetic, solar feminine activation within you, the reader. In my research, I learned more about the capacity to learn, activate, and ignite through mapping, which I describe as plugging into the energy field of another who embodies this energy.

To this end, I requested that nine women answer three questions; each of them is currently activating the solar feminine within. These powerful and varied responses provide you an opportunity to map to the solar feminine energy that each writing embodies.

Plug yourself in.

• *Charlon Bobo*

How is the solar feminine downloading in you?

The solar feminine is downloading in me as crystal-clarity, dramatically heightened intuitive knowing, and certainty in discerning the next appropriate action step in every moment. My sense of spiritual hearing is becoming highly acute as I listen and respond to every inspiration—every subtle nuance of divine guidance.

My physical body is being reconfigured on a cellular level as this process refines my entire soulful self. As a result, I take plenty of naps! Our 3D bodies aren't currently wired for such an influx of awakening, and yet all of that is changing right now as each of us willingly embraces (even the possibility of) ever-higher dimensions of experience.

What changes have been required of you as you move into the solar feminine?

As I move into the solar feminine, what I require of myself (because the solar feminine does not impose anything on us) is three things:

1. **Unquestioning willingness to take action based solely on the directive of inner knowing.**

   I am being trained in an esoteric mystery school and my guides instructed me to "operate in alternate dimensions of time and space." So, even though I still have no concept of what this means or how it works, I'm doing it! As a result, something dramatic has shifted. I feel it and this alone is my confirmation of truth.

2. **Willing desire to change any and all aspects of my life to align with my marching orders.**

   To embrace, embody and emanate attributes of the solar feminine at least initially, I had to do everything counter-habitually. This was an inspired, strategic method of moving from where I was to where I am now. It was imperative to set aside all systems that previously supported and defined my experience on this physical plane. To be an active part of my own evolution, I had to actually do things differently, so I started with everything!

3. **Full presentness in every moment.**

Every moment is fresh and new, requiring an in-this-moment response. In every moment I take the time to allow the inherent wisdom and the guidance of that moment to reveal itself to me. In the past I would have imposed by own will, which completely evaporates the inherent gifts moments contain. When I listen to the inspiration of the moment right in front of me, it whispers everything I need to proceed with certainty that that is the perfect, appropriate action for the highest benefit of all parties.

What are your "sacred marching orders?"

Sacred arching Orders are evolutionary; they shift, morph, and change with the passage of time. My sacred marching orders right now include igniting the solar feminine for the evolution of humanity, and embodying and emanating the intended true form of primary relationship between women and men so the masses can map to it. There are other mini-marching orders, but those are the most prominent.

I take my sacred marching orders seriously, but there is also much room for fun on this unique journey. As an example, I wear my vintage combat boots as I go about the everyday business of my life. They are a powerful visual reminder to myself of my mission, and they look so fabulously silly with some of the outfits I wear. Regardless of the intensity of my mission, life should still be fun!

• *Katherine Brandon*

How is the solar feminine downloading in you?

When I think of the Solar or Active Feminine, it brings to mind a female holding a sword right in the center of her body, the pointed tip facing the sky. Grounded to the earth and sure in her purpose, this woman is fully in service, ready to embrace whatever is needed.

As I meditated on this image, I thought about feeling called to battle, but not wanting to engage in violence. I felt the pull to take a stand and fight for something, to risk, to push forward, to act. At the same time I felt a nagging voice in the back of my head saying that you can't be a peaceful person and engage in battle. Then I thought of Gandhi and that voice was put to rest.

As I considered this further, I began to realize that we are meant to be the sword—the tool of protection and action in this world. We are to be centered, balanced, sharp, and willing to slice through our complacency and re-engage with the planet, our selves. and with each other.

What changes have been required of you as you move into the solar feminine?

It has been important to actually spend more time connecting to the Source, slowing down, and making sure I am connected. And this inevitably means spending more time with other like-minded people in community.

What are your "sacred marching orders?"

To connect with The Mother through nature. To have the courage to not only speak the truth, but live the truth and stop the violence in my own world so that it may spread to others and the planet.

• *Lorna Brown*

How is the solar feminine downloading in you?

The biggest and most apparent aspect I have noticed is in dealing with physical situations where trusting my intuition and inner guidance is paramount. I have made life-enhancing decisions, which are totally contrary to accepted standard practices but have required me to take a stand and move against what "authorities" would counsel. It is proving successful.

What changes have been required of you as you move into the solar feminine?

My life requires that I totally listen to and trust my intuition and follow that inner guidance, which equates to three major concepts: listen, surrender, and trust.

What are your "sacred marching orders?"

I have been guided and spiritually supported in writing my memoir from the perspective of an awakening spiritual soul, and to create a new workshop in connection with this work about women (or men) stepping into their true power and essence.

I meet regularly with four separate small groups of empowered women who support each other on their journeys, another group that is creating a teaching concept regarding the sacred mysteries, and another group that is creating regular ceremony connecting the sacred feminine and masculine into the new humanity of Earth.

• **Victoria Hanchin**

How has the solar feminine been downloading in you?

I have become more and more deeply attentive to inner impulses of intuition. I call this "Sacred Listening." As I tune in, I receive guidance. Sometimes the guidance is so clear and compelling; it shows me a path of action, a vision, or a project. Once this guidance shows up with such inspiring force, I feel compelled into action.

This guidance feels like a volcanic force coming through that propels me. When I am not in daily action aligned with this guidance, I feel restless...it feels like trying to cork a volcano, and that just doesn't feel good! So, I deeply desire to follow where its energy wants to take me. I feel centered, inspired, and grounded when I am in service and communion with this guidance.

It is like the Creator and I are passionately co-creating a magnificent epic movie, and I can't wait to discover what will unfold next in our collaboration. I get that I am an integral and necessary part of the Divine Production Crew!

What changes have been required of you as you move into the solar feminine?

I have been compelled to grapple with the "shadow" aspects of myself. This includes confronting the part of me that hates being in the public eye, the part that believes I can't do it right, the part of me that doubts, the part of me that feels more comfortable playing small, the part of me that wants to hold back. It is amazing. All these layers of self-imposed limitation!

So I have learned to distinguish when I am operating from the habitual conditioning of my "default office"—that disempowering inner space of my limited ego-ic identity. I realized that I cannot be magnificent and co-creative, living from the limiting beliefs of that "default office." I learned how to step out of that limiting, disempowered identity.

One of the ways I did this was to create a ceremony, focusing on an Altar of Surrender. This was not a passive surrender, like, "Oh, whatever," or "I give up." It was a fierce surrender, using imagery of the snake as a symbol of death, rebirth and transmutation. The snake is also an ancient symbol for the Goddess. I created a visually powerful altar, and declared out loud my intention to surrender to my most Infinite, multi-dimensional, Master Being Self, in the service of the most magnificent, infinite purpose that I came to this planet to accomplish.

I recommit to this sacred surrender as needed, reading the Hafiz poem that is part of this altar: "If your love letters to me are true, dear God(dess), I surrender to who YOU keep saying I AM."

My life literally changed the day after that ceremony, expanding into that larger Divine Identity and Divine Service! And it has been expanding ever since.

What are your "sacred marching orders?"

My "sacred marching orders" are to serve as a Mouthpiece for Divine Mother and Mother Earth, on behalf of humanity's shift into our divinity and our co-creation of a New Earth of Love, Joy and Unity.

This divine assignment is expressing currently through a process of Sacred Listening that has led me into aligned action in these four areas:

1. Assisting humanity to unplug from the frequencies of fear and re-wire into the frequencies of joy and unity

2. Harnessing the power of the awakening feminine to shift humanity out of the love of power into the power of love

3. Exploring heart-based sacred partnership in a relationship that allows collaborative sacred listening within a context of our union of divine masculine and divine feminine beings

4. Unifying the Indigenous and non-Indigenous peoples, to restore our capacity to experience living from our original, whole, Indigenous Soul, as we reclaim living in a sacred manner with Earth and All Our Relations.

• *Jan Hill*

How is the solar feminine downloading in you?

It has manifested as profound and inspired energy that is directed towards planetary change. It is fueled by a sense of urgency, which is nurtured by a deep sensing that all will be as it is meant to be, that the sacred earth and the divine spirit will cradle each other, and we will somehow make it through this period of transition. I am stronger than before. I walk taller. I send my energy out into the world, in service of change and celebration. I work hard. I am not afraid to die.

What changes have been required of you as you move into the solar feminine?

The most significant change I have observed lies in my deepest sense of physical knowing that in each action, each interaction, each thought, each feeling, each moment, I have the opportunity to create in a new way. Every action, interaction, thought, feeling, and moment counts. It is all about NOW being in service of the future. I speak out. I plant gardens—metaphorically and literally. I care for creatures discarded by others. I look people in the eye and ask the hard questions of myself and others.

What are your "sacred marching orders?"

To protect—with fiercely loving conviction—the creatures of the planet.

• Nina Howard

How is the solar feminine downloading in you?

I continue to receive information on a daily basis through a variety of sources that I draw in. For instance, I am drawn to find a stream of sunshine coming in my window and have the rays touch my body for some time. When this occurs, I feel like I am in some sort of communion as if I am downloading blocks of information. After just a few moments of time with the sun, I feel a deep peace come over me. My awareness draws in information about how the divine feminine has been suppressed. I am very aware that I am gaining in personal mastery of who I AM. The power of being feminine allows me to make changes that I could never have made just a few short years ago.

What changes have been required of you as you move into the solar feminine?

I laugh out loud reading this question! It brings to mind a young suitor begging for my sexual attention. Before stepping into my power, I would have surely buckled under the seduction. I simply cannot give away my core energy nor can I allow another in unless a complete vibrational alignment is taking place—along with honoring and love. The change is a deeper honoring of who I AM.

As I progress through this cycle of growth—moving to my personal mastery—a contradiction exists within me. As I become stronger, purer and more defined in the mastery of who I AM, I feel softer, more capable of loving deeply and less conflicted, but the energies must be honoring.

What are your "sacred marching orders?"

My sacred marching orders are to be a Wayshower. I call myself an Inspired Wayshower.

In 1986 I became acutely aware that I came here to assist the planet's Ascension, thus my own. I spent years preparing myself with outer knowledge (books/classes) and inner knowing (meditation/contemplation). In 2007, my codings were activated and I knew, from the depths of my being, that it was TIME. I had received my marching orders! I began preparing to tell people about the transitional shift through writings, lectures and my website. My orders are to bring awareness to my circle of influence and any others that a major shift is about to occur in the multi-verse which includes humans, plants, animals, Mother Earth, as well as other star systems, ETs, and galaxies. We are all being prepared for a systems upgrade! If we can get past fear, we can ride the wave to a higher frequency and move beyond the limitations of this Earth Matrix. Honoring the light within and coming to terms with the darkness is the ticket. Wouldn't NOW be a good time to begin the journey home?

• *Sura Kim*

How is the solar feminine downloading in you?

I feel the sacred feminine coming through most strongly in my throat and solar plexus chakra. It manifests as a higher awareness of expressing and asserting my truth and what I perceive to be true; having the courage to express freely and openly without hesitation or doubt; having the courage and receptivity to hear others' truth and be in an open, honest exchange with anything that arises.

What changes have been required of you as you move into the solar feminine?

The biggest change and call I feel as I step into the solar feminine is "stepping it UP." Taking the experience, knowledge and tools and offering them to the world in the greatest way possible. Dancing, meditation, movement, and self-healing help greatly to move and catalyze the energy of the sacred feminine. Our wisdom is contained within our cells—our very being.

Nurturing the self, taking walks, resting, and treating ourselves with love are all part of the divine feminine. Nurturing is one of the greatest forces in the world.

What are your "sacred marching orders?"

My sacred marching orders are to cultivate presence in each moment, listen deeply and act on intuitive guidance, do what I can with flow, grace and love, and be myself.

• *Kathe Schaaf*

How is the solar feminine downloading in you?

In some ways, I have always been in touch with my solar energy. I have no problem being focused, organized, and efficient. People have often reflected that I get so much done in a short period of time, that I can keep track of lots of information and know how to work hard. I am grateful I learned those skills growing up in my family.

Around my 50th birthday, I began experiencing a longing for something deeper and more meaningful in my life. I simply began following my intuition and soon found myself in a hive of women passionately engaged in supporting the arising feminine energy on the planet. This is when the Solar Feminine really began to work in my life. I began experiencing a surge of energy and creativity that is both vast and incredibly focused. Like the hawk circling high above the landscape, I sometimes have the vision to see large patterns yet also act with precision to take the required next step.

My skills of manifesting and doing are more grounded in passion and informed by Spirit. As the feminine aspects flowed in, they softened the sharp edges of my solar energy. Intuition and inspiration relieved me of the need to have all the answers and being part of a circle of trusted women was so much more fun than alone pushing boulders up the mountainside with my forehead.

What changes have been required of you as you move into the solar feminine?

The biggest change has been the requirement to surrender to something larger than myself. I am both more effective and happier when I can get out of my own way and follow the flow of grace. Sometimes that means being still and waiting for inspiration or movement. I have learned how to appreciate the pauses and the mystery of this journey we are on together.

I've also learned new tools of discernment, acknowledging when something does not feel right for me. It is painful when I say, "Yes," to the wrong things. Truth-telling seems to be another requirement these days. Transparency is one of the qualities of the new paradigm and it is important for me to have integrity with my co-creators and my community. And I have learned gratitude. I am more aware every day of the blessings and grace in my life.

What are your "sacred marching orders?"

I love this phrase—though some days my marching orders are to sit still and watch the hummingbirds visit the purple sage in my yard.

My divine assignment is to gather women. Z Budapest, one of the founding grandmothers of the modern goddess movement said, "The knowledge comes from gathering... and gathering and gathering." I have been gathering women since 2002, when I was one of the founding mothers of Gather the Women. Since then I have gathered women and women's organizations in many different configurations.

Like many of us, I am in a constant process of learning, practicing, experimenting with new forms and structures. My latest assignment has become more precise: Women of Spirit and Faith seeking to gather spiritual women for a collaborative exploration of leadership and power. I know I am listening well to my sacred marching orders because this work makes my heart sing.

• *Krysten Wall*

How is the solar feminine downloading in you?

I sense more and more feeling movement in the first three chakras, pleasure in being on this earth, feeling of being connected to the earth, nurtured, and fed by cycles of the natural world. I have found more joy in living, eagerness for each dawning day, steadiness of mental focus, emotional resilience in performing the tasks of life and the challenges as they come. There has been a striking clarity to perceptions of life, especially in seeing others' needs, confusion, cares, or burdens. My willingness to be present with others feels free, quick, and unquestioning. Knowing what I can do to support them is apparent to me, naturally and easily. Physical strength and health are steady, not depleted by activities.

What changes have been required of you as you move into the solar feminine?

I have had to let go of my own story, as if it were released to fly on its own, without my rehearsing or ruminating. This feeling I have reminds me of the saying, "It is what it is." I feel mildly curious, as if my story is just another human drama, like so many others, but I no longer feel identified as the particular carrier of this or that stress. I have had to find my own lightness, to travel beyond the confines of the person that I thought I was. The change has been really a shift in focus so that I am open to other energies or intelligence, so they can move through me.

What are your "sacred marching orders?"

The only activity that is worthwhile has become increasingly clear to me. It is to open my heart and bring whatever comes through to whomever is present. It seems so simple. I see the role of the human self as in service, I suppose, to step aside with its myriad preferences and allow the greater work to be accomplished. So, whatever is presented to me to do is in the service of the flow of the universe. I may still do gardening or psychotherapy or helping with grandchildren. However, the way it is done is in context of the movement, or flow of all of life toward wherever it needs to go.

Joan of Arc Warrior Energy
by Kathleen McIntire

[Note from Patricia: This mighty adventure was sent to me as I completed Sacred Marching Orders. *I found it fascinating that Kathleen's experience occurred so soon after my own solar awakening. The energies are strong and being activated quickly. I've included this piece because it is a stunning example of a solar feminine activation.]*

The fierce feminine is erupting in me as what is needed on the planet right now. I have four signs in Aries: Sun, Jupiter, Venus, and Mercury. In shamanic astrology, this archetype is the warrior Joan of Arc, the crusader for truth. All four signs are in the second house, doing all of this for the earth, for the Mother.

My Aries has been dormant and there was a huge awakening to this Joan of Arc Aries energy starting on January 26th. That day marked the beginning of a 12-year cycle of connecting to my deepest personal truth. It was

time for the Joan of Arc within me to awaken. I began
watching Joan of Arc movies and absolutely loved how I felt
as I resonated with her fierce spirit.

The Birth of Joan of Arc Within Me

We were in the midst of a huge snowstorm. When it
snows this heavily, I am snowed in because I live on a
private road that is not maintained by the county. I decided
this time I would try something different. I contacted my
neighbor who was in Maui. Her driveway connects to the
road that is maintained and plowed by the county. Perhaps
I could park in her driveway.

Getting to her home in 10 inches of snow was an
adventure in itself. Let me just say I had to be rescued and
helped when my truck became stuck. Getting there was like
Mr. Toad's Wild Ride at Disneyland. I realized I should have
backed in so I would be facing out. But alas, I was parked
for now.

The following day I went back. I saw two neighbors out-
and-about. Chains. That was the key. I could keep myself
from being snowed in every time with chains! So I got to
my truck and started shoveling snow. I had on ski pants, a
parka and high outdoor boots. The snow was quite light
and I shoveled a path for both tires and also the berm made
by the snowplow. The truck didn't seem to appreciate or
care that there was a nice little path made just for it to back
up. Obviously, it had other plans. It jumped to the left in
deep snow and wouldn't budge. Out of the truck with
shovel in hand, I dug another new path. Again the truck
jumped to the left as I tried to back out; into fresh snow
and not budging. Again, I shovel. This went on and on.

At one point I nearly made it out but would have hit the
stone posts at the entrance. My usual pattern would be to
attempt this for a few minutes and then get help. The

damsel in distress, there has always been someone to
rescue me. Not this time. NO. I was doing this one alone.
No help from a man or anyone else. The moment I got there
I knew in every cell of my body this was about claiming
that Joan of Arc part of myself that had been asleep.

For three hours of continually moving in the wrong
direction. Not only was the truck jumping left but I was
also losing ground, going steadily forwards instead of
backwards. I stopped and paused. Again thoughts of hiring
someone to come get me out with a winch and a truck
flashed before me. Defeat. No, that was not an option.
What would Joan of Arc do? Certainly she wouldn't be the
damsel in distress waiting to be rescued. She was guiding
and inspiring vast armies to victory to save France from
being taken over by the English and to get Charles crowned
king.

I had to stop seeing defeat. I called on the energy of Joan
of Arc. I got out and surveyed the situation instead of trying
to do the same thing over and over and over, to no avail. I
saw that I had cleared so much space which was now all
on one side of the truck. I thought of possible strategies
Joan of Arc would implement. Then I thought of the chains
in the back of the truck! YES, the chains! People were
getting around with chains.

Once I had helped a friend with chains, I knew you had
to back into them or drive forward onto them. I didn't know
how to connect them once they were on, but I would deal
with that when the time came. More shoveling. The snow I
had driven over and over was now ice. I did the best I could
with the shoveling. On my belly I laid the chains in the
exact right position. I backed up just enough for the tire to
fit perfectly over them. I got out and wrapped the chain
around the first tire in delight until I saw that it was 10

inches too short. Why were there chains that didn't fit? Maybe they were for the other car!

Still, the chains would give needed support and dig in as the tire went over them. Over and over I would shovel and move the chains a bit and keep trying to back up. The truck was like a horse with an inexperienced rider, determined to go the direction it wanted. I would have to shovel snow in front of me. There was so much shoveled on the one side but I didn't have room to maneuver the truck to get it there.

I shoveled like Popeye after eating another can of spinach. Next attempt, once again to the left and into the snow. Nothing was working. I started to swear, then remembering Joan wouldn't allow the men in the army to swear. How was she going to help if I sounded like a drunken sailor? No more swearing. Again, I asked what would Joan do? She prayed. Everything she did came directly from her hearing and seeing the plan of the Divine. I prayed to the supreme being, to my guides, Mother Mary, Jesus and Mary Magdalene and also to Joan and to her saint, Saint Catherine. I got out and looked at the situation taking everything in. It was getting dark and I was soaking wet with melted snow and sweat. More shoveling. My back ached. I kept going as hard and fast as I could. I began envisioning the sweet success of succeeding. I visioned it with all my being.

I jumped into the truck crying out, "Okay, it's time for a miracle. The sun has set. It is now or never. Let's do it!" I almost made it; the stone gate was in the way and would have hit it though. Okay, that was the best attempt in hours. Rubber was burning, smoke rising in the air. I went forward again and started rocking the truck slowly forward and then back again, and again, and again, chains having been placed over the ice. Once more and we took off like a rocket, out of control but going backwards and making progress. Now I had to plow the rest of the area behind me. I needed to back all the way out onto the road and then back in so I could go forward in 4-wheel-drive when it was time to drive somewhere. I shoveled the rest of the snow, got in and the truck obeyed like a faithful servant.

It was done. I hadn't wimped out. I had just re-wired a pattern of my entire life: the belief that a man would always be there to rescue me. This time, through the Divine, I had rescued myself. I felt so empowered. As I walked home in the dark, dripping wet, with at least a quart of water in my leather gloves, an old gospel song flooded into my head with the phrase, "Get down upon your knees and pray." So I did, effusing gratitude. I was so happy. The next day I woke up feeling muscles I didn't even know I had. Oh, the sweet, gentle, beautiful ache of it all.

In the Western worldview, we tend to see the feminine as the lover and the mother. We have forgotten she is also the shaman and the warrior. It is drummed into us that we need to be nurturing, loving, nice, and caring. We put our needs on the back burner and take care of others. If we aren't happy, or in a good mood it is assumed, if we are in the appropriate age range, that we are PMSing. If we are passed that age, we are simply an unbearable bitch. The message is if we continue with that behavior, no one will want to be near us. We will be ostracized, abandoned, and alone. The relentless societal messages are: be a nice, good girl and follow the rules that are in place.

One day, we finally wake up and realize the rules in place have been put there by people in power who want us to remain asleep to the truth, by those that want to manipulate us, by people who are fueled by greed and want power over food and resources and this planet.

It is time for we as women to wake up to all of who we are—to the shaman with access to wisdom in other realms and to the divine. It's time to wake up to our warrior energy. The feminine is fierce!

In the story of the Donner Party there is one part that is little remembered or told. When things looked bleak and hopeless, the men got depressed. It was the women who stepped up and had the courage, the belief, and the power to make it through. It is women who endure the pain of childbirth and act like protective mama bears when raising their children. It is women who have a deep power to prevail and persevere.

Now is the time for us as women, to step up into our Joan of Arc Warrior selves and connect with our voices that have been lost—at least temporarily. It is time to roar. It is time for the battle cry of a new world that works for the benefit of all life—a world in which resources are made available for all and each human has the freedom to pursue his or her greatest gifts and make their unique contribution. It is time for the Aquarian age, and we have been placed here now to make this happen. It is time to listen and get our marching orders from the Divine and then go forth to create this new world. Individually and collectively, we say, "No more," to the way things are. We say, "YES!" to a new world with new rules of equality for all and we are here to create it!

"*Exponential expansion is like fireworks popping.*"
– NENIE BEANIE

6

Sacred Marching Orders

In researching and writing *Sacred Marching Orders*, the working title was *Sisters Stewarding the Shift*. I never fully settled into that title and now I understand why: the first title was almost completely lunar feminine. I actually knew nothing of the solar feminine when I began writing. *Sisters Stewarding the Shift* feels like a peaceful float down a lazy river. It's beautifully appealing and certainly carries a high vibration.

Sacred Marching Orders is more like white water rafting. Clearly, relaxing is not part of this energy.

At this transitional time, single-pointed, clear powerful action is appropriate and necessary. To that end, receiving and responding to each of our own sacred marching orders is the way that we play our parts fully and dynamically in creating a New Earth.

We'll float later. Now is the time for clear, inspired action.

Marching Orders from the Still Small Voice Within

To receive our "marching orders," we must develop a heightened attunement to our inner voices. Many refer to it as the "still small voice within."

Women receive and accept a constant onslaught of "marching orders" from the outside: wear this; weigh this; look like this; do this; care for this; clean this; accomplish this; and for God's sake, keep smiling and don't complain. We are no strangers to "marching orders." Another word for "marching orders" is "directives." We live our lives responding to external directives—the marching orders of others.

The Stepford Wives was a movie that depicted a frightening example of the robot-like qualities of conforming completely to external directives. As we acclimate to marching orders—or directives—from the outside, we assimilate them and mandate ourselves to follow the directives that have now been internalized.

Geneen Roth calls this internalized rule-maker "The Voice." Some call it the critical parent. This is not to be confused with the "still small voice within." A helpful guide to assess the difference between The Voice and the "still small voice within" is that The Voice usually carries a quality of "should" or obligation, and makes you feel wrong, small, or worse about yourself.

Let's clearly delineate the differences between your inner voices.

Another way to describe this distinction is to say that we are externally or internally referential. Being externally referential is focusing on events, things, or voices that exist outside of us, mirrored in the world of materialism. Being internally referential is being aware of—and responsive to—the subtle voice within.

THE "VOICE"	THE "STILL SMALL VOICE WITHIN"
• Makes you feel worse • Feels heavy • Is harsh • Carries a "should" or feeling of obligation • May be frantic, insistent or obsessive • May be critical • May be angry • Plays the role of victim; pitiful and helpless • Judges you • Leaves you feeling tired • Drains your energy	• Comes when you're quiet • Comes when you're alert to your active inner world • Has a feeling of "popping up out of the blue" • Is often surprising • Is clear and concise • Leaves you feeling as if you just "know" something; you are certain • You feel clear when you hear it • Is often divinely inspired • Energizes and ignites • Is the voice from which we receive our "marching orders"

We are all internally referential when we are born. We know when we're hungry, uncomfortable, or mad. But as we become immersed in the socialization process, our connection to our own inner voice diminishes until it is virtually non-existent. Learning to be internally referential again, takes practice.

To receive your unique "marching orders," you must reference your inner wisdom, listen to the still small voice within, and take action in alignment with the guidance provided.

Marching forth is staying strong, staying in the moment, and staying connected to the still small voice within.

– NENIE BEANIE

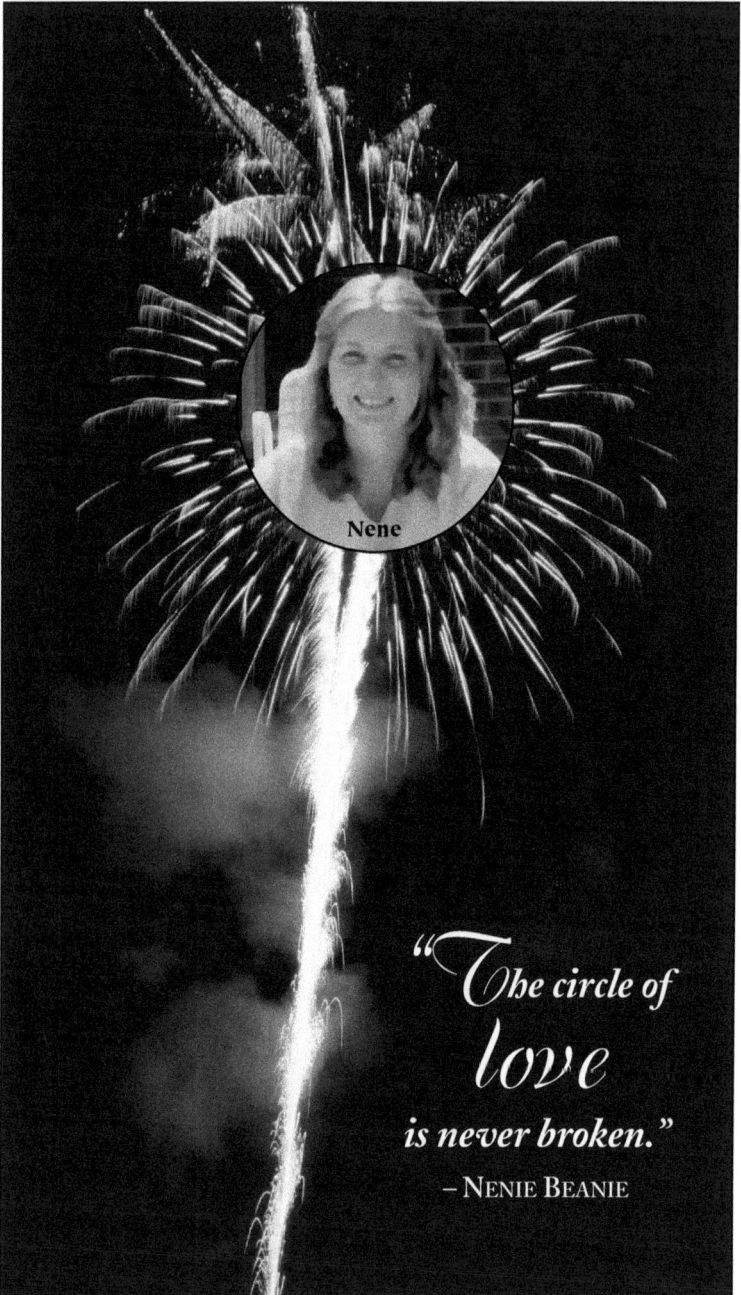

Nene

"*The circle of*
love
is never broken."
– NENIE BEANIE

7

Solar Flares

The following interviews are conducted with women I refer to as "solar flares." They are shining examples of the embodiment of the solar feminine.

These conversations—Solar Exchanges—provide an energetic vortex into which you can plug to activate your own power. These connections provide a map for the new woman on the New Earth, which is being ushered in by the feminine. Each interview is infused with this powerful energy.

As you read each Solar Exchange, know that it contains an energy field that is available to fuel the power of the solar feminine within you. Each of us has a choice as to how powerfully we respond to this call.

Now is the time, and we are the women.

So, with great pleasure, I invite you to:

SALUTE THE SOLAR FLARES!

Introduction to Nenie Beanie's Solar Exchange

When I began rewriting *Sacred Marching Orders* and moved powerfully into the energy of the Solar Feminine, I came to wonder where my sister Nene's energy would fit in. I knew it had to be included and maybe even featured because her energy had been a catalyzing force for me since we began communicating three days after she left her body and began residing in nonphysical realms.

Now, I realize that she fits here—leading the parade of the women I call Solar Flares. Several years ago, a seer told me that Nene's energy was a fountain of Light, like a geyser that ignited my work. As time passes, I find this to me more and more true.

So with great pleasure, I introduce you to my sister, Nenie Beanie, Solar Flare Extraordinaire.

Nenie Beanie's Solar Exchange

PAT: Nene, I feel a lot of pressure here because I'm tapping into your energy with the expressed purpose of publishing and featuring this writing.

NENE: Let go of that knot in your stomach. You know we can't connect well like this. That knot is fear, and fear lowers your vibration. You need to be in a high vibration to connect with me. Remember that card you pulled this morning? Different dimensions are just energies vibrating at different speeds. Relax. I've got the vibration to carry us through this interview. See how you're starting to relax?

This is the first thing I'm going to talk about that has been being brought into your awareness—The power of "fierce surrender."

Fierce surrender is a powerful energy of the solar feminine. When I was diagnosed with cancer and I said, "Not my will, but Thy will, whatever is best for the children," that was fierce surrender.

When Joan of Arc went charging directly toward her fate and cried, "I am not afraid, I was born for this," that was fierce surrender.

So, in my role as your first solar flare, I offer you the power of fierce surrender.

Okay, Nenie Beanie, Ms. Solar Flare, what's next?

You women must stop being afraid of using battle terms. If you had any idea of what is occurring in the non-physical world, you would drop this fear like a hot potato. This is the time for the warrior feminine, the Amazon energy. How do you win a battle when you're afraid to even use the language?

When I was in form, I had a very sweet personality, but when it came to my spiritual path—as I marched toward my death those 14 years—I was a fierce warrior. Warrior energy is about intensity and commitment, not violence and destruction. The military action that occurs on the planet now has been completely distorted by patriarchy. This is not about being a warrior, it's about being a bully. The United States holds all the weapons and used them in brutally unfair ways. That has nothing to do with battle or being a warrior.

The fierce warrior stands strong in the face of opposition and she calls on enormous internal resources. You speak about the activation of the lower three chakras. This is real and relevant.

The fierce warrior plants herself in Mother Earth, asks for guidance and strength from the Divine Mother, calls on all her passion and will, and uses all of her power in the service of all life.

This is the energy of the fierce warrior, and this is what is required now.

Okay, Nene, this is wonderful. I have a feeling you have one more solar feminine quality you want to tell me about.

Yes. It's the fireworks you love so much; the image of fireworks exploding from within and igniting the fireworks in others. That's the energy of exponential expansion we used to love to talk about. Remember how we loved to say, "It's expanding exponentially"?

That's what is being shown to us with fireworks. It is the magic that is occurring now of exponential EXPLOSION being activated within by the solar feminine and then igniting others and watching them explode with the energy of the solar feminine.

Now, that's fireworks!

Fireworks are the perfect symbol for the reality of exponential expansion—the multi-faceted, multi-colored streaks and stars of light that explode from the center with a giant POP.

This is also the experience of hearing popcorn pop. It starts with one, then another, and then it feels like each one is igniting another and another until it builds to a crescendo that is so far removed from that first little pop.

That is the energy of exponential expansion—fireworks and popcorn—images and sounds. These are the language of spirit. See how alive and energized these images feel? This is the energy that is occurring in unseen realms now. Make it visible within yourselves, and as you activate yourselves, you ignite it within others until it becomes a powerful crescendo fired by exponential expansion.

Thanks so much, Nenie Beanie, ending this interview with the words "exponential expansion" is perfection itself.

Enjoy the ride.

> "*Exponential expansion is like an explosion.*"
> – NENIE BEANIE

Introduction to Liza Nuremburg's Solar Exchange

Introducing you to my friend Liza as a solar flare makes my heart sing. I have many wonderful women friends, but I absolutely *adore* Liza. She does not belong to the powerful circles of women with whom I connect on a regular basis. And the only spiritual or metaphysical book Liza ever read were the ones I wrote.

Reflection and deep internal listening inform me that my enormous admiration for her is because she is the embodiment of love in action. Her father was a sociology professor who wrote his PhD thesis about Martin Luther King, Jr. Liza and her family were among the small numbers of Caucasians who risked their lives marching in the South during desegregation.

I imagine that her powerful experience of love in action was the training ground to develop her capacity for being a powerful force in standing for love. This is the energy she embodies and this is what makes her a solar flare.

I envision her deceased father watching over her. He is proud. He did well. Liza is a model of a woman acting on behalf of love.

Liza's Solar Exchange

We build trusted relationships with our sisters despite outdated cultural pressures.

Pushing through the old…

PAT: *Womens' focus on beauty—especially in a competitive way with other women—is the dark side of the feminine. It's one of the ways that we women diminish each other, as well as ourselves. Please talk about this. You are so good at cutting through all that somehow, and even in milieus where women might be comparing and judging each other, you find a way to align with a woman so she becomes an ally rather than a competitor. I know this is something you consciously do, and I'm wondering if you'd be willing to talk about the whole phenomenon.*

LIZA: For me, it was an awakening at a very early age. I grew up in the 1970s when girls had very few opportunities to excel in sports or anything like that. I was pretty, so I became a cheerleader and a pom pom girl. While I was happy with that, I also began to feel very isolated because I couldn't trust people. I was always in competition with girls who were supposed to be my friends.

In the first year of college, I decided that I would choose trust and friendship over the competitive aspect of female relationships. And that was difficult to do. I wasn't met with a warm welcome; "Oh yeah! Let's all have a trusting, carefree friendship!" Instead I was met with suspicion. It took a conscious effort to stop living competitively and to reach out to other women with trust. It was difficult, and it remains difficult to this day.

I have a deeply-engrained sense that when I walk into a room, I need to instantly scope it out and size up the competition. It's a primitive thing, and I have to actively work against doing it.

Feminine competition probably came about culturally by the necessity to get our essential needs met. But now we're competing for the guy, the job, the best mother award, and more. And when women compete with each other, they help to shape each other's inauthenticity. It's exhausting to be around people who you don't trust, with whom you can't be authentic. So I made a conscious decision in college not to live like that.

Yet to this day, when I walk into a room in my corporate position, if there's another female there at my level, the instinctual "size her up, oh boy, oh boy, this could be bad" kicks in. I can feel my face harden and myself becoming more bristly and prickly, and I always sense that from the other women as well. In fact, there are women who won't speak to me, or even come near me, if they think I'm the competition. They just stare.

I actively tell myself to take a step back from my feelings, to approach the women, to reach out to them because very, very infrequently will other women do that. I'd say 90% of the time when I do extend myself, I'm met with relief, huge relief. There are some women I write off as impenetrable, and then I just back away gently. But most of the time I'm met with sincere gratitude that I've made the effort.

Building sisterhood anew...

When I was a social worker in a people-oriented industry dominated by women, it was much easier to reach out and be engaged in a more authentic way. When I began to work in the male-dominated corporate environment, it was more difficult again. It took my current boss to say to me, "How is it that you manage to befriend males and females? How do you do that?" before I thought about it.

I noticed that some strategies I use are initially superficial, but they work to calm down women, to build trust and make friends, and to connect so we can talk. For example, I compliment the way other women look. It's following the old social work adage…you meet them where they are. So, if I see a woman who's looking nervously over her back, smacking her lips, digging at her purse, messing with her hair, I walk up, say hello, introduce myself, and immediately compliment her. It puts her at ease to talk to me.

Step by step through the years, I've made deep, deep friendships with women, and I trust women much more than I did. There's nothing more fierce and more powerful than building relationships between women. When women become friends, the level of intimacy becomes such a bond, you see yourself doing most anything.

You can see yourself raising her children if she's no longer around. You can see yourself being nursed by her if you have cancer or if you're dying. You can see yourself trudging along and helping her do things that are very difficult for her to do.

I personally don't have that kind of trust and that sense of intimacy with men because they're more scary. For me it's very important to have strong women in my life and to have relationships that I can trust and love, so I work very hard at it.

When you're busy competing with somebody, and you distrust them immediately based on your assumptions, it's like they're hiding behind a mask and you're helping to keep them there. If you push through the mask, you realize that they have pain, sorrow, all the same things that you grapple with, and it's so much more powerful to grapple with those kinds of issues together than it is to do it alone. Women have saved my life. I've said that time and time again at various points in my growing through the years. Women have literally saved me from myself and from situations that were out of control.

I'm virtually breathless as I listen to you. This is so powerful. I'm thinking about the patriarchy we live in, and I've said frequently that womens' roots were severed. Before, we were deeply connected with the earth; our roots were deep in the earth. We were connected with animals and herbs and plants and trees and each other. That's the way we lived.

When humans started growing crops and could accumulate surpluses, cultures shifted. Opportunities increased to acquire and accumulate property and to hoard it; our roots to the earth were severed in service to this trajectory, and female access to resources became limited. Competition might have actually been very survival-based at that time.

I have a friend who had a vision of how in these early times, women started maneuvering for the most powerful man—the man who could not only provide access to resources, but also protection and safety. Perhaps, we had no option but to attach to men like parasites. That speaks to some of the shadow aspects of the feminine that have developed in our misogynistic patriarchal culture.

I also especially wanted to share that as I listened to you talk about the relationships of women, I felt your energy shift from competition to connecting! It was powerful, and models what's possible for us.

I have to acknowledge my mother here, because she wasn't one of those women who pushed female competition. Other young ladies I watched had mothers that told them, "You get out there and you get the biggest and best award; don't trust her." Fortunately, I didn't have that constant feed to my brain.

Living in two cultures simultaneously…

I remember an experience I had in my freshman year of college. I liked school, and I was paying less attention to my physical self, less of the primping, more letting days go without makeup, that kind of thing. I like to say, I turned poor and had to get a job.

I applied to be a cocktail waitress, and one of the things you had to do to get the job was prove that you could look good in the outfit. It was one of those tight 1970s Danskin outfits with high heels, red and trashy looking, but it was a hotel lounge and that was the trend then. I thought, "Hmm… I can either do that, be in that culture, or I can stay poor."

So I put on the outfit, got the job, and then spent my days in college trying to be authentic and not competitive, and my evenings engaged in the old way so I wouldn't be poor.

It occurs to me that you had to play the role to gain access to resources. I was just reading recently that until 1964, a woman could be fired for being married.

Fired for getting married, fired for getting pregnant. And I think it was probably up until the early 70s that stewardesses, as they were called back then, could be fired for putting on weight, let alone getting married. I mean, stewardesses were not married, period.

I laugh at how I still want to look like a flight attendant. I've found that when you tell on yourself by saying, "Oh my God! I have the biggest zit on my forehead… I can't function!", women trust you more. They understand, laugh, and say, "Yeah, I know what you mean!"

Other women, depending on their generation, might want to look like a Barbie or a Crissy doll. But I laugh and I say, "I want to look like a flight attendant." And it absolutely makes my heart sing when young ladies say, "Eeeew! Why?" I think, "Yeah, you're getting it... not too glamorous, is it being a waitress in the sky?" But they don't have the experience of looking at those women and being told they're the best, or the prettiest. "You should want to do that. Look at their lives. They're sophisticated. They're glamorous."

Though I do my best to find the spirit of cooperation with women nowadays, it continues to be difficult.

Becoming aware of the pressure...

These seem like scrambled thoughts, but they're the gut feelings I've had for many, many years that I haven't really conceptualized. I know you'll be able to frame and articulate them well, drawing what is needed out of my ramblings, so that other women can understand and relate to what I'm talking about.

What you just said is really interesting... "drawing out of your ramblings."

Remember our recent conversation about what we women do to ourselves? We dismiss. We discount. We diminish ourselves. These things that you say are not only NOT ramblings, they're powerful articulations of this enormous shadow aspect of being a woman in this structured culture.

And shadow work always needs the integration of the disowned aspects of the self. When the truths of this story are told, women will say, "Yes, it's true," and see it in themselves, in others, and bring it out into the light—to consciousness. And that's how the shadow dissipates. So this is important and powerful information!

There's one more thing I want to say. This terrible, terrible distortion of who we are has been created by the dominant culture in the service of womens' powerlessness and subservience.

And then it's further acculturated, passed on by the subservient elements of our culture to allow the continued suffering. If you're a mother and you want your daughter to have the best, you will encourage her to follow the culture because that's what gets her the best result.

I might even say it this way... In our culture women are encouraged to betray other women. This is a powerful observation! I believe it begins with women being encouraged to view each other as competitors rather than as human beings. Viewing others as competitors allows us to dehumanize them, which is really a betrayal of human life itself.

That's true. And women betraying women undermines feminine values, and power as a whole.

Absolutely. It's natural for females to be in deep relationships, attentive to the most intimate details of real life, with children and family and other women. Although our system of competition may be wounding both women and men, there is something about the back-biting and isolation for women that is particularly oppressive.

It's important for women to reach out to other women; to be open, authentic; to listen and try not to judge. Humor is important, as well as the willingness to be the first one to do the reaching. Teach your daughters and your sons to reach out, and be gentle with them, because the cultural messages they get are compelling and overwhelming.

> " *Y*ou are the center of the universe, but then again, we all are."
> – NENIE BEANIE

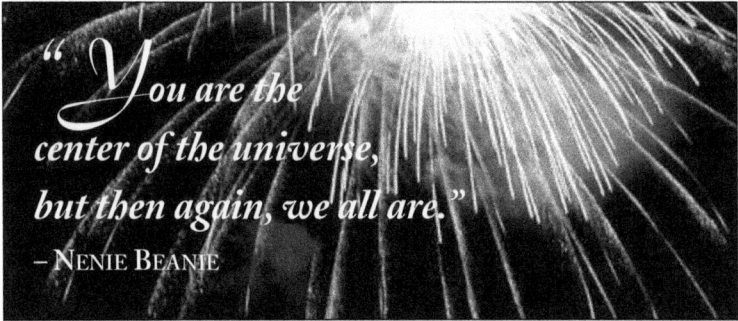

Introduction to Sharon Riegie Maynard's Solar Exchange

Sharon Maynard introduced me to concepts that shifted my life. Since our first meeting, I hear these awarenesses spoken of frequently. The drama unfolding on our planet involves much more than we can see with our physical eyes.

Sharon identifies herself on her website in the following way, "I am Sharon Maynard, a radical mystic, radical seeker, and a shawoman. She describes a mystic as someone who seeks answers from beyond conventional sources of information.

She writes, "A radical seeker is one who is not satisfied with standard answers, but delves even more deeply into what others have forgotten, ignored, buried. Shaman value the energetic relationship between all energy forms, elements, and divas in the circle of life. Sharon owns her power and is confidant in her exploration in other dimensions. Sharon is a fierce, fearless explorer, which positions her perfectly as a solar flare.

Sharon's Solar Exchange

Our nature as women is to be powerful, recognizing what needs to change, and declaring that it be so.

Restoring true purpose

<u>PAT</u>: *In writing* Sacred Marching Orders, *I'm asking women about what they're doing, how they perceive the role of the collective feminine in planetary awakening, and how they see their piece in that unfolding. In response to that, what are you inspired to say?*

<u>SHARON</u>: The sense of women awakening has been around for a very, very long time. It's been the total focus of my work since about 1997; women are asleep, and must wake up. Until that happens, the world will not shift.

When I began my work, I had a simple knowingness—a certainty—but didn't understand what it meant. It was only as I worked with individuals, watched what happened in their lives, and asked more questions of my spiritual guidance team that my understanding came.

First, I asked, "Do women as a gender have a specific purpose on this planet?" Then, "Do men as a gender have a special purpose for this planet?" All the while, I doubted a positive answer would come, but I was told that both genders do indeed have specific agendas. A gender, just like an individual, comes into form with a specific overall focus and a purpose. That was a surprise to me.

So the question, then, became, "What is the purpose for the female gender?" And the answer that came was power: the power issues, using power, leadership, being the leader, taking charge and moving things forward. And I asked, "Well, then, what is the specific agenda, the assigned vibration for the gender of men?" and my guidance team said, "It is love; it is nurturance."

I said, "Well... we certainly have that one backwards!" So I come from this knowingness about women waking up maybe differently than some.

I understand that women as a gender have a specific purpose to work with power in appropriate ways or identify powers to be used in appropriate ways. And since I come into this lifetime in a female body, I have personally faced this agenda to work with power, as well as my own personal issues. I have walked a path of uncommon awareness.

I was eventually made aware that the earth itself has a special purpose, and the purpose isn't to be a school room. It isn't a learning space. I see that we are trying to shift back to earth's original purpose, the original purpose for the gender of female, and the original purpose for the gender of male. Only then can we accomplish what we intended to accomplish when the world was first called into being.

Without that shift, we will continue to play around in the effect of the entrapment, the false systems that were put into effect very shortly after the earth was created. Talk about the sleeping beauty. The sleep state for women happened very shortly after the planet was called into being, and we were forced into sleep intentionally. And you notice, it's not a story about men being put to sleep. We have no fairy tales about men being put to sleep. It's the women who were put to sleep, and that's because it was the woman's divine assignment to lead this world into a state of sovereignty and realignment to our divine vibration. That was our role.

Empowering ourselves without anger…

This is an extraordinary understanding. This time that we're in, the womens' leadership being activated, being on this path since 1997. It must be fascinating for you to watch what's unfolding now.

It is, all the more so because I was not involved in 1970s feminism. I was a mother, shepherding diapers. And I was very asleep. I was very socialized into NOT playing my true gender role.

When I was finally called to work with energy as the mystic shaman that I am, I could see this in myself. I knew that when women were put to sleep, they became unaware of their own connection to power and purpose. When women in the 60s started to wake up, they did what women do when they begin to see things differently. They went from accepting powerlessness to being angry.

Women get angry when they recognize and get glimmers of how disempowered they have been. At the time, I saw traditional counselors advising women to stay angry, because if they didn't, they'd slip back into accepting powerlessness.

Many of these women fought to have their own identity, their own voice, and be accepted. They became powerful in the work world, making a name for themselves. Yet, all too often even these women were eventually kissed "awake" by a prince charming who became abusive—hammering away at them as they lost connection to their power in their personal lives.

When I saw these patterns in the women I worked with, I'd keep asking, "What's in the way? What's more? What don't we understand?" I kept searching for deeper answers than those we had.

I discovered that women don't have to get angry. It isn't

a necessary step anymore. We can just begin to say, "This isn't okay for me." From there, as we do healing work, we become more and more in touch with how we feel about ourselves and our lives, more authentic, and we get clearer about the underlying webs of false stories we've believed about ourselves. We reestablish a connection to our innate dream.

We all come in with an innate dream, ability, and skills that we are here to activate. That very skill and divine ability draws to us the resources we need to support us. In other words, we are attracting the resources that support our souls. In their healing women, begin to feel this, and then to step forward with their dream—their individual dream of contributing to the world.

Awakening all the way...

Still I ask, "What is missing at this point in the womens' movement—in the womens' awakening?"

As we awaken, we reclaim awarenesses of former times. We go back to where we wove the gardens. We go back to the times when we were warriors holding space. But we have not yet gone back to the time when we were given the divine assignment to clean up this planet. And that's the awareness we have to reach. We're still in process. We're still working our way to that place.

There are women at all stages of the process. There are some women who are still struggling in powerlessness. There are some women who say, "I'm uncomfortable here," or "Wow! I love what you're doing." They find books to read or classes to attend. or people to mentor them, rather than stay in powerlessness or angry reaction. Some women are awake, and they have an authentic voice and a sense of themselves. They bring projects, activities, and organizations forward. And even beyond that, there are women who are really willing and ready to hold hands and network. That's a higher awakening because in that awakening we will be required to heal all our collective genetic and history as women—what's held in our mass psyche, including our experiences from the Burning Times. That will be required of us, so that's a higher form of awakening.

But an even higher form will be awakening to the fact that we are here to discern power that is life-affirming, and how power that destroys can be eliminated.

Wow! This is fascinating. Everything you said resonates in me so strongly. One of my friends shared with me an ancient Mayan teaching that suggested that women were to be the leaders. And it's intriguing how you describe a continuum, almost a scale of waking up—where women who have discovered their calling and their impulse to connect with others, are then called to heal the roots of their separation.

That's it...

Very cool.

And even though I didn't understand it completely, I've worked very successfully with that continuum model. Looking back, it fits in so many ways, and the impact that it's had on womens' lives has been amazing.

I've helped women who came to me basically saying, "I'm through with my marriage; I even want to throw out my sons." They experienced their first step of awakening as anger with men. They saw the lack of support and the lack of understanding.

And the entitlement.

Some of them saw those imbalances in their homes.

Other women saw it more extensively in the workplace. I'd say, "Okay, let's realize that whatever's going on in your world is you. Let's focus, first of all, on your stories. What are the stories that have gotten you to this point? Let's track those stories."

Of course, they were totally committed to that because I attracted women who were ready to move forward and absolutely committed to taking responsibility for their part. I have seen it over and over again. When the woman stays with her healing and transmuting and looks at what keeps her trapped, etc., six months later she reports that the men in her life are falling all over themselves to make her happy.

The power of environment, of discernment...

That's amazing!

Yet, the man's loving behavior isn't submissive. The role of the man isn't meant to be submissive. He's a very powerful force. His true role from the beginning was to nurture and stand for possibility. It was to hold the vision of possibility, and then to bring that from the crown chakra into the heart's energy and nurture possibility.

That's what men have been cut off from; so when they wake up, they don't wake up with anger. They wake up with huge pain—heart pain—and that's why a lot of men do not choose to wake up!

But when women shift into their authenticity, they begin to say, "This is the kind of environment we need for the family: order, touches of beauty, because this is what we need to accommodate and encourage abundant and joyous living." That's correct use of power.

A woman waking up calls for the correct energy in her

space first, and then she aligns with what that means for her and her family. The men come in to offer their insights and muscle in loving service to absolutely make sure the correct energy happens. That's how we are meant to work together.

I have been given information that can help explain why this natural alignment has been so disrupted on earth.

There are energy societies who have invaded our space many, many times, over the eons while we have been in our fear. And it is absolutely to their advantage to crush women because women are the ones who can sense them. We are the ones who intuitively know something's not right here. When we know something's not right here, and we have the power and the respect to be heard, we say, "Something's not right here. I don't know what it is, but I need this space cleared out of everything that's not good for my family." Such a command causes spiritual beings to do that, to literally take any invading energies and send them back to their homes.

As long as these energies exist among us, we will have the world we now have. As long as women do not use their natural power to safeguard our spaces, these energies will impact us.

So these energies enter where there's fear.

They let fear and chaos invite them. That's the law. Whatever vibration is present, more of that energy is invited to present itself. If you hold a peace vibration, you attract peace. If you hold a fear vibration, you attract fear.

So the fear is our own. It attracts energies that are not our own, that stay hidden, and are the very ones that women were intended to identify through their sensitivity. Instead, these invading societies have locked us away in a state of denial, pretending that they don't exist.

There are a few of us now who understand our situation and are clearing the planet of these invading energies. That frees the rest of us to pay attention to clearing our own resident, fear-filled patterns. And women learn, once again, to be powerfully sensitive and protective of the human family's environment.

Wow! I was raised Catholic, in a very very dysfunctional family. There was a lot of fear, a lot of chaos, and a lot of anger. I've worked really hard to reject all that. So the idea of invading entities is a really difficult concept for me. I don't know how to relate it to my personal experience.

That's partly because having no power, the easiest thing, really the only thing to do, was to just walk away from awareness of them. That's actually how we've survived to this point. It's only been since about 2004, and especially since 2007, that we've had the right to face the situation, and say "no" to it.

Think back, Pat, to a time when you experienced a really awful situation; go beneath the behavior. It might have been a priest speaking hell and damnation, or your father being aggressively controlling. Even the Bible says you will know the truth by the fruit.

I guarantee that if you go back to that time, letting yourself be in touch with the energy underneath, and ask the energy three times, "Are you of my family's light?" the answer "no" will come to you. At that moment say, "Then you must be taken back to your home planet," and the energy will go. This is what women were intended to be able to do with invading energies that we recognized, but we have not had the right to call it out. That right was taken from us shortly after the planet was created, when we lost the female mission.

That's the power we are now regaining as women. And you're right. It's been too huge to really integrate into our understanding. I received a channeling from Mother Earth in 1997, in which she said, "There's coming a time when you will be able to take off your masks. You accepted powerlessness. You accepted everything they put on you as women, as my sisters, because you needed to, in order to survive. If you fought them then, they would have destroyed us. You became submissive by choice. You stepped into denial initially because you were forced there, but now you've stayed in denial by choice."

The questions I wondered were, "Can we survive? Can we prolong the life of our greater family on this planet until there is a time we can step out of denial and be free?" Now is that time, since about 2004 and 2007 more extensively.

So each of us, who listens to our inner guides, feels how to step forward.

A continuum of women's pain...

I felt a new level of personal activation in 2008. Around the turn of the century, I traveled extensively, working with adults, focusing on women. I lived on a retreat center for two years in the Napa Valley in California. I worked on the land, wrote and did a moderate amount of teaching, including some sessions.

I thought I would be working in a major way for women in 2003, but my guides said, "No. You're going to help your daughter create a pre-school for children." So from 2003-2007 while I helped my daughter, I was called to an inner mode, where I did my deep work. I had one particular friend who worked with me.

Then in January and February of 2007, it was time to cut back on pre-school and move toward my outer work again.

I remember Constellations of Hope, in November, and the Mayan Calendar speaking of the influx of galactic information on the following weekend; November 12, 2008. I have only been doing my work again since then, coming out of a four-year purifying hibernation time before that.

Let's talk about the Constellation of Hope gathering a bit. I was told that a First Nations' woman asked a Caucasian woman, "Why do you always take our rituals? Don't you have any of your own?" And somebody said, "No, we don't." It occurred to me that we don't because our roots were severed in the Burning Times. This story seems a perfect expression of where we are now—re-establishing those roots.

I was at the Constellations of Hope gathering, and it was a First Nations' woman from Canada who was offended by a Caucasian woman drumming, and she said something like, "You're taking everything." And some of us even laughed as we acknowledged that indeed we didn't have our own rituals. I'm Swedish and I don't even have a Swedish pancake recipe!

How disenfranchised we women of European descent have been! And what I got out of the Constellations event is this: First Nation woundings, as well as their efforts to integrate them, are more recent than those of European women. They have a lot of hurt and anger that's not resolved, but they have begun to turn that around.

By comparison, the pain of women with African heritage is very raw, especially those directly from Africa because the wounding is still happening in the present, right now. Their pain was so in the now, that they couldn't even voice it without tears to each other, and they couldn't even begin to share it with the larger group.

So again I saw a continuum of pain—really fresh, now pain in our sisters with African heritage; pain being assimilated and turning itself around in our First Nation sisters. And then I realized that the sisters with European ancestry have pain that is so far in the distant past, repeated and repeated then, until we have become so assimilated, we don't even know we've assimilated this pain as our normal state.

It looks like we're free when we have no glimmer of being free. We are grabbing onto our sisters' ways, and perhaps we do need to have our hands slapped, so that we do indeed "re-member" our own ways.

In 1997 or so, I had an experience with a Native American fellow who makes documentary films. He gave a speech, talking about his film and his intention to go to all the indigenous tribes of the planet, and record their prophesies to see the similarities. He spoke of one tribe, one village in Borneo, that had been invaded by another indigenous culture. The invaders had come with the intent to totally destroy the village, to kill and massacre all the major leaders of the village, and take away whatever captives they felt could be assimilated into their tribe. This they did.

Twenty-five years later, three young men met in a South American city. As they spoke to each other, they recognized that even though they were raised in different places, in different tribes, they had all come from that village. Their spark was to go back to the village and "dream awake the bones of their ancestors." They went back, committed to living in the caves where the bones were placed and dream awake the wisdom, tradition, everything that was in the bones of their ancestors, and restore their tribe that way.

I went up to the speaker afterwards and told him I was so touched by that story. He looked me in the eyes, and he said, "When are you going to dream awake the bones of your ancestors?" "What?" I said. And he responded, "The women."

I feel that that is exactly what my work is about. I'm dreaming awake the bones of our ancestors. For me, my piece is to go back to the original bones—the original mission for women—power used correctly.

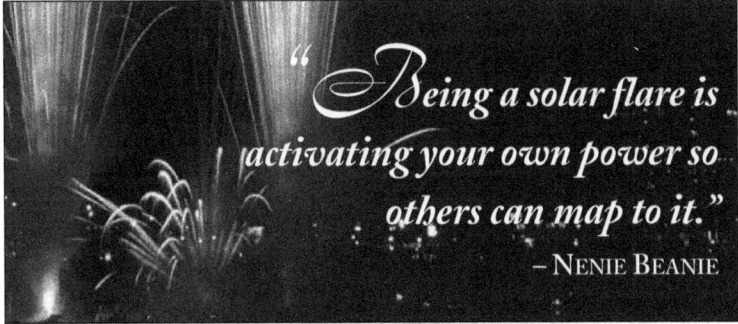

> " *Being a solar flare is activating your own power so others can map to it.* "
> — NENIE BEANIE

Introduction to Lucia Rene's Solar Exchange

Lucia Rene, author of *Unplugging the Patriarchy,* is the embodiment of the solar feminine. She writes, "the solar feminine (is a) style of femininity that my spiritual teacher cultivated in his female students."

Lucia has integrated and demonstrated this energy so effectively that it serves as an energetic gridwork for others to map to. She is like an electric power station—holding for us the energy of the solar feminine, ready to be ignited within us.

As each of us ignites that spark within us and then carries that flame for others to be activated, we create an explosion of energy that bursts forth in the creation of this New Earth that has been predicted for thousands of years.

Lucia's interview carries the strong energy of the solar feminine. Enjoy it, and allow that spark in you to be ignited.

Lucia's Solar Exchange

**We unplug from our conditioning and
stand in our own power to create a
collective field for change.**

Impeccable warrior…

**<u>PAT</u>: The work you do is so extraordinarily powerful, and
you're playing a significant role on the planet right now. I'll
start by asking you to say whatever it is you feel moved to say
to begin our conversation.**

<u>LUCIA</u>: Well, I do think it's an interesting role. Of course,
it's not a special role. We all have gifts that we come
bearing. We all have skill sets that are much needed at this
time of awakening on the planet.

But my role is a unique in that it's the role of a warrior,
and there aren't that many women on the planet right now
who really resonate with the lower chakras or energy
centers in the subtle physical body. Those are the power
chakras. Sometimes you'll see a woman in politics or a
world leader who does, but mostly, it's a lost art.

I was trained by my spiritual teacher, Rama, to be what
he calls an impeccable warrior. While he was alive,
working with his students, Rama focused on the
enlightenment and the empowerment of women. In fact,
that was his primary goal. He turned out a group of women
from his program that really know how to access their
lower chakras and do what I call "standing in their power."
My role is simply to embody that, to hold that energy in a
way that women can map to it, or that it's communicated
when I walk down the street. It's a fearless warrior in a
feminine body which doesn't mean that fear doesn't come
up occasionally. But it's bringing back what I call the solar

feminine, the active creative, passionate side of existence, the yang, within female embodiment. So that's the role.

What comes up for me as I listen to you, Lucia, is that when I attended your workshop, and you did the energy work with me, I felt so much activation of my lower three chakras. It sounds strange to use these words, but it was like a heaviness or denseness. It was a solidness that I never experienced before in my lower three chakras. Your concept of "mapping" feels significant to me.

There are two things we feel when we tap into that as women. One is that it's just a lower octave. It vibrates in a different way than the upper chakras, than the heart energy center or the wisdom chakras that are further up, the third eye and so on. So it's not bad or good. It just vibrates in a much deeper more, resonant way.

The other thing we feel as women when we begin to tap into those energies is how much garbage we've collected there, how out of alignment they are, how much is stored there, and how many processes are stored there. We've been forced over the last 5,000 years of this male-dominated, fear-based patriarchal system, to take those energy centers, those three energy centers, the root, the second chakra, the naval chakra, and set them off limits.

The root is about survival, the second chakra about birth and creativity, and the naval [solar plexus] chakra, which I place right below the physical naval, is pure power. That's the power of the mystic or the magician, the ability to get things done in the world. We've taken those off limits, and crammed everything down. We've stuffed every urge to act in a powerful way down into that area. So when you activate that for a woman, you activate access to all that baggage that she has to clear.

I'm mesmerized by what you say and the way that you say it. It's so clear and powerful, and my reaction is beyond words.

My hope is that your reaction will be to stand more in your power.

I am. And I keep saying that Lucia is the real deal. That is the point I want to make… the authenticity. And at the same time I want to acknowledge you, I'm alert to my propensity to create a white shadow.

What do you mean by white shadow, again?

My white shadow is projecting my positive qualities onto someone else and elevating that person. People don't usually say "dark shadow," but usually when they talk about shadow they're talking about a disowned aspect of the self, a quality that someone doesn't want to claim. I guess this is also true of white shadows, but they point to the positive end of our polarities. I just realized that there are reasons I don't want to claim positive qualities.

Marianne Williamson says that our biggest fear is the fear of our own power. It scares us to death because for 5,000 years we've been counseled not to go there.

That's been my experience in this lifetime; there was a mandate that I not go there. I imagine it's true for many women because patriarchy permeates our family systems as well as our adult relationships.

Finding balance…

Yes. As women, if we've gone toward power, we've been told we need to develop the masculine side, and the masculine is so laden with connotation for us. What is it to be a man? Strong, unfeeling, always pushing your emotions down, never cry, be the bread winner. Then we go out as women, put on business suits, and become successful in the world. There's nothing wrong with being successful in the world, but we lose something with this strategy.

That's why I changed the words. I discarded the words "masculine" and "feminine" at some point in my research and replaced them with "solar" and "lunar." If you advise a woman to reclaim the solar, not the masculine, it completely removes the emotional charge; the male association. It takes away the connotation of masculine because the solar is simply the active, the passionate, the creative, and the lunar is the receptive and the nurturing. It's the moon, the Yin quality.

We have the lunar down. That's what we've been programmed to think of as feminine. But we need to reclaim the solar. Of course, there are some of us who have been very programmed as the solar. I was. I had a very masculine upbringing, so I had to reclaim the lunar. But whichever one we have to reclaim, the time calls for balancing the solar and lunar—the masculine and feminine—within ourselves.

And the solar is really reclaiming and reactivating those lower three chakras.

Exactly.

This is obviously crucial since we're so naturally designed to connect deeply, to root ourselves into Mother Earth.

Yes, and the inclination to be of service. Throughout the history of the patriarchy, if a woman worked in the world, it was with a charity. She worked for the benefit of humanity. That is using the third chakra, the naval chakra.

Mother Teresa, as we said at my workshop, was a magician. She used that chakra, but within the context of the Catholic Church without going against the precepts of the Catholic Church. Most women—when they first step on a spiritual path—practice karma yoga, which is the yoga (or spiritual practice) of service. That's natural because women are intrinsically more powerful than men. They intrinsically resonate with the vibration of the power chakras, those lower three chakras. So it's very natural to know how to get things done, to move out into the world and serve humanity.

It's only after some time of being on a path of karma yoga that women graduate to mysticism, which is the study of power or energy—the way energy works in this world. That's really when a woman comes into her own, when she studies pure power or pure energy because women intrinsically know how to wield power in a balanced way. In other words, they know how to pull the energy of the upper wisdom chakras, how to balance power with the wisdom and strength of the heart, and then to wield power through the naval chakra.

Being a human being in a female body…

As I'm listening to you, I feel so much more activation and energy in my naval chakra and in my listening field. Please talk about the 12 female archetypes you spoke of in your workshop, and also the positioning. You used the metaphor of places on a chessboard. I think there's something very significant about the vision you hold that connects women to certain archetypes. I'm interested in what you want to say about that.

In the project that I did, "Unplugging the Patriarchal Female," we identified 12 patriarchal energies, that relate to the seven personal chakras within the subtle physical body, and the five transpersonal chakras—chakras that are for the most part located outside of the subtle physical body. As we focused on each of those chakras, we put names to them, and discovered that they were classic archetypes handed down from a matrilineal time.

So there are 12 beautiful archetypes that came down to us from this matrilineal era, maybe 6,000 years ago, that have been fractured, polarized, and corrupted by the patriarchy. For example, there is the classic archetype of the healer—she who can heal through energy or through sound or sight. When that archetype is fractured and polarized we get "she who buys into the patriarchy" and "she who rebels." The buy-in nurse is she who takes her directives from a male doctor, while the rebel is she who rebels against that cubbyhole, becoming something more akin to the witch midwife who was burned at the stake during the inquisition.

Another example is the classic archetype of the tantric lover, which is second chakra energy. The second chakra is about birth and creativity. Women used to be able to transmute consciousness by having sex with someone. Certain women had the gift of being able to relate to someone sexually and literally flip them into alternate dimensions; they were often priestesses at temples. The patriarchal buy-in of this is actually the role of "wife." It's the only acceptable way to use our sexuality. When we rebel against the patriarchal expectation of being a wife, we become the whore.

Most women have had experiences with all 24 bastardized cubbyholes that are the polarized remnants of the original archetypes. It's like putting a round peg into 24 square holes and seeing if you can make it fit again and again.

I think most women gravitate towards one or more of the 12 original archetypes. Quite naturally they know, they have an affinity: "I'm a healer," or "I'm a seer," or "I've always been psychic," or "I'm a mother," whatever it is.

But my goal is to help women come into a place where they can own all the so-called bad experiences that they've had for hundreds of incarnations—to own them for the gifts that they are. If we go into each of those archetypal energies, tapping into the energies of those lives and those various experiences, then we bring them back online so they can be reconciled. This is what's needed: To balance the 12 polarities, and restore wholeness to the original 12 archetypes within ourselves.

The goal, then, is that we embody all 12 archetypes; that we become the sacred number of the divine feminine which is 13. So, we embody all 12 archetypes and the Divine Mother herself. This is what we're capable of; this is what we want to express in our day-to-day life. This is an awakening to our potential as a human being in a female body.

Toward a field of resonance, enough is enough...

And we're at such a unique time in human history, with direct access to so many energies. Please say something about the urgency of the times along with their fertility; their potential for expansion.

Absolutely! It's an extraordinary time, and my view is that women are on the front lines of consciousness. We are in the midst of a balancing act. We're balancing the masculine and the feminine or, if you will, the solar and the lunar. The way we begin, of course, is within ourselves because we have both the masculine and feminine within, even though we take embodiment as one or the other.

It's clearly the masculine energies within the collective

that are creating the wars, famines, rapes, violence, and oppression. The feminine is very much on the front lines and there is a progression to what is happening. Always the group that is oppressed must rise up, must take back their power, must reclaim their integrity.

The slaves in the south had to rise up against the slave owners. It wasn't the slave owners who came and said, "We're so sorry. We're going to undo this. We're going to do it right now." So, we as women cannot expect men to ever bring us to the table as equals. Women have to take that first step and simply do what I call standing in our power. This doesn't mean that we stand against something or for something, but that we stand in balance in the place where those two polarities for and against come to rest.

This is not to say that we don't act—that we don't act for something and against something. This is dharma—what we do in the world. Of course, we protest. Of course, we stand in opposition to war. But if we're standing in balance, in integrity, in our own intrinsic power as women, this means that the personal self has been moved out of the way so the divine feminine can come through. Actions that come through us in this way are exponentially more powerful than personal actions.

So my seeing is that women must collectively be willing to reclaim their power and stand in it. When that happens on a large enough scale, it will create a resonance on the planet—a vibratory field—an energetic field. If you assign words to it, it resonates as "enough is enough." That's where we're going. Enough is enough. We all know that, but women must get their arms around the fact that we have not only to stand in our power, but also to collaborate with each other in doing so. This is where the resonance comes in: enough of us standing, and that energetic force field becomes very, very strong, and there's a point that we will reach.

It's as though the patriarchy is a giant monopoly game. We don't know how long it will take or how many women must be standing, but all we need is enough people to stand up and say, "I no longer want to play this game."

The patriarchy exists because we give it permission to exist, and in my view there's nothing wrong with the patriarchy. It's been a hard 5,000-year learning, a difficult learning, a painful learning, but we have been learning about power, and issues around power, and that includes abuse of power. So we are in a time now at the end of this patriarchal era, what the Hindus call the Kali Yuga; the time of greatest darkness, meaning it's very difficult to see clearly at this time on the planet. Things are so churned up. At this time of the Kali Yuga, a phase transition needs to occur.

The patriarchy is inside of each of us as I describe in my book. We must unplug our energies from it, pull the curtain aside... you know, revealing the Wizard of Oz... and see the inner workings of the patriarchy. Then we must say, "No more, I won't play this game anymore."

Unplugging our energies doesn't mean getting off the grid or riding your bicycle or recycling, although there's nothing wrong with any of those things. It means to energetically unplug, and women are on the forefront of that movement.

Women know they're on the forefront of that movement. They've been called by the divine mother whose energy is extremely present on the planet and by mother earth. Many, many women have heard that call. It's amazing how many women, despite all odds, are standing around the world in developed countries, in undeveloped countries, and creating this resonance. So eventually, we will come to the point where it flips.

At that stage, men sensing this enormous crescendo of female power will naturally have a reaction to it, but this is healthy. If men go into reaction, into a process, they will be able to bring the masculine and feminine to rest within themselves. They'll bring it into balance. But they have to have something to react against. So women must make the first move, and men must react. Then they have to do the clearing work. Of course, there are many men on the planet already doing this clearing work, but not enough. But every little bit helps—women working on themselves, men working on themselves.

My objective is to bring this whole transition in for a more graceful landing, to help this Ascension happen in a more graceful way. If we play it all out on the physical plane, the patriarchy coming unraveled will be quite painful.

Most people don't understand these principles—the mechanics of consciousness. They don't understand that you can go into a process within yourself, and examine the reaction that you're having to something. You can work with that polarity within yourself, bring it to rest, and then you're no longer attracting it outside. So if enough of us do the work, we can help the rest of humanity.

Yes, and as more and more of us do the work, it makes these energies more accessible for those who are coming along.

Exactly, because we don't have to understand it with our minds. We don't have to talk to each other, communicate, or be on the Internet. We don't have to do any of that, although, of course, it's helpful to meet together and exchange ideas. But the Ascension or the awakening happening between now and 2012, is happening in terms of consciousness. It's magic. We've entered a time in which anything is possible.

Is there more that's important to say?

There's one more piece, and it's a very inspiring piece. As a therapist, Pat, you know the inner work, and women standing in their power, the work of men clearing the emotional body and being willing to reclaim the heart and the lunar. It's not easy work. A person really has to go into those areas of the unconscious, to be willing to move into their fear and deal with it. And more and more people are willing to do that now because their backs are against the wall. They have no choice.

But the truly inspiring thing to me is that all of the energies on the planet are working in our favor. Mother Earth is cycling up. This really is her show. It's really her Ascension process. We just happen to walk upon her and Mother Divine is here in force to help with the birth of this new consciousness. Her energy dominates the planet at this point.

So if women and men can tap into those two things—the cycling, the ever increasing vibration of mother earth, and the readily available refined energy of the divine mother who's here to midwife the birth—then our own personal Ascension process goes much more easily.

The way to move into the Ascension—to really take up residence in this new world, the new paradigm of consciousness which is readily available now—is to move into the energy of the heart, to think with the heart, and move power through the heart. In any area of your life that you're holding on, you have to open your hand and let go, and just see what spirit has for you; what spirit has for you at this moment.

We've entered a time when we really have to be in the moment. When we fall back into the moment, then we have mother earth's Ascension. We have Mother Divine's energy. We have spirit. We have so many beings who are here to help this Ascension process available to us. We can let spirit act in and through us. That's the ticket to the new world.

Those are magnificently beautiful words. That's the ticket to the new world. The ticket home.

Yes. The ticket home.

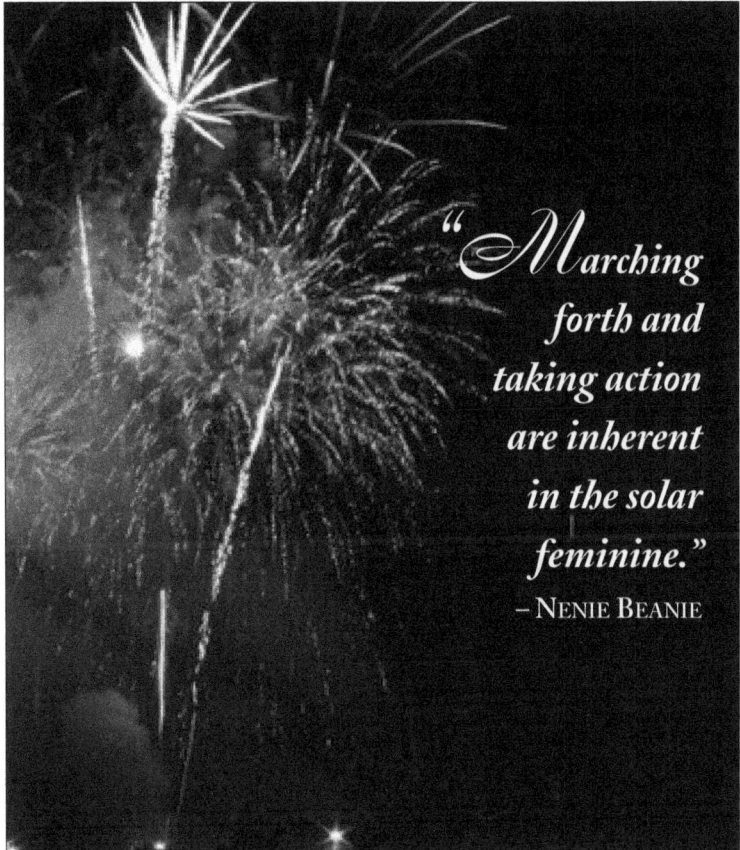

> "*Marching forth and taking action are inherent in the solar feminine.*"
> – NENIE BEANIE

The Ticket Home

What is the **TICKET HOME?**

The **TICKET HOME** is
remembering
what we have forgotten.

The **TICKET HOME** is
*knowing fully &
completely*
the words that Jesus said,
"Ye are Gods."

The **TICKET HOME** is
knowing that
each of us
holds within us the power to
*transform the darkness
within ourselves into
the Light.*

The **TICKET HOME** is
knowing that we have
*the power to return
the magic*
to the natural world.

꙳

The **TICKET HOME** is
knowing that as we
communicate with nature,
She responds to us
with her wisdom.

꙳

The **TICKET HOME** is
honoring the sacredness
of the web of life.
The **TICKET HOME** is
*activating the spark of
the solar feminine*
that lives within us. As we do this,
we ignite that spark within others, catalyzing an
energetic explosion like the most magnificent
fireworks display imaginable.

This will demonstrate once and for all time how powerful
we really are. And we will remember and behave as the
sons and daughters of Mother Divine, that we really are.

Boots on the Ground

You've just read a beautiful description of "The Ticket Home," home to a New Earth; a powerful description of the promise, "on earth as it is in heaven." We're not there, yet. In so many ways, the journey has just begun.

Now is the time to tune into that still small voice within, and listen intently for your marching orders.

BOOTS ON THE GROUND

It is the perfect moment to join forces and salute our leaders.

BOOTS ON THE GROUND

In service to the Divine Mother and Mother Earth, we march forth powerfully.

BOOTS ON THE GROUND

We are solar feminine women. We are united, guided and we are here to reclaim our power in service to humanity and the planet.

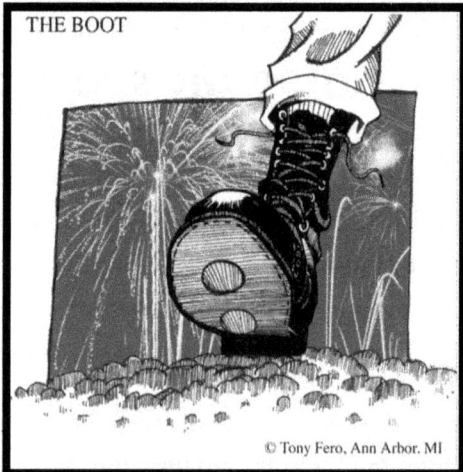

THE BOOT

© Tony Fero, Ann Arbor. MI

www.ingramcontent.com/pod-product-compliance
Lightning Source LLC
Chambersburg PA
CBHW052004090426
42741CB00008B/1546